A Pilgrim's Guide to

THE LA
OF ST PAUL

Greece Turkey Malta Cyprus

Raymond Goodburn and
David Houseley

Pilgrim Book Services Limited

© Pilgrim Book Services Limited
David Houseley and Raymond Goodburn 2001

ISBN NO 0-95325-112-8

Published by Pilgrim Book Services Ltd,
P O Box 27, Woodbridge, Suffolk,
England IP13 9AU

Cover and Text Design by Fielding Design Ltd
Production by Book Production Services
Maps by KPG Ltd

Printed in Great Britain by Polestar Specialist Colour Ltd

Acknowledgements :

Ilustration of St Paul Mosaic on front cover and photographs of South
Cyprus by courtesy of Stephen Page. Photograph on Page 20 by courtesy
of Temple World Travel. Our thanks also to the Tourist Board of North
Cyprus for facilities made available to us.

Cover Picture: Mosaic of St Paul in Veria, Greece (Stephen Page), printed in reverse

Contents

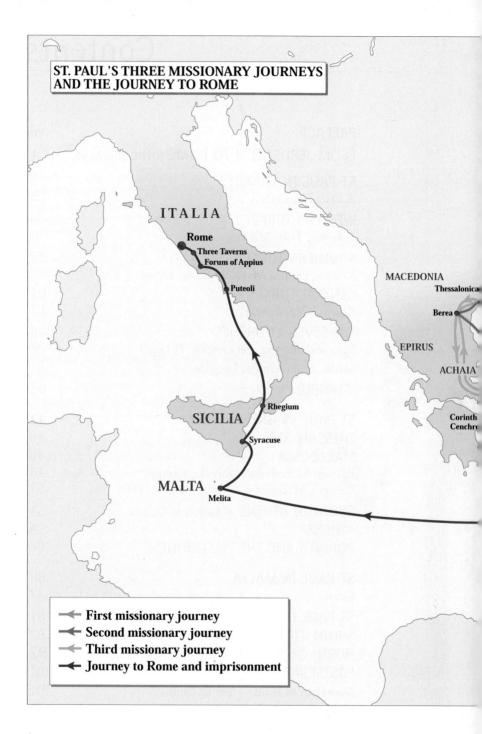

ST. PAUL'S THREE MISSIONARY JOURNEYS
AND THE JOURNEY TO ROME

ITALIA

Rome
Three Taverns
Forum of Appius

Puteoli

MACEDONIA
Thessalonica

Berea

EPIRUS

ACHAIA

Rhegium

SICILIA

Corinth
Cenchre

Syracuse

MALTA
Melita

◄— First missionary journey
◄— Second missionary journey
◄— Third missionary journey
◄— Journey to Rome and imprisonment

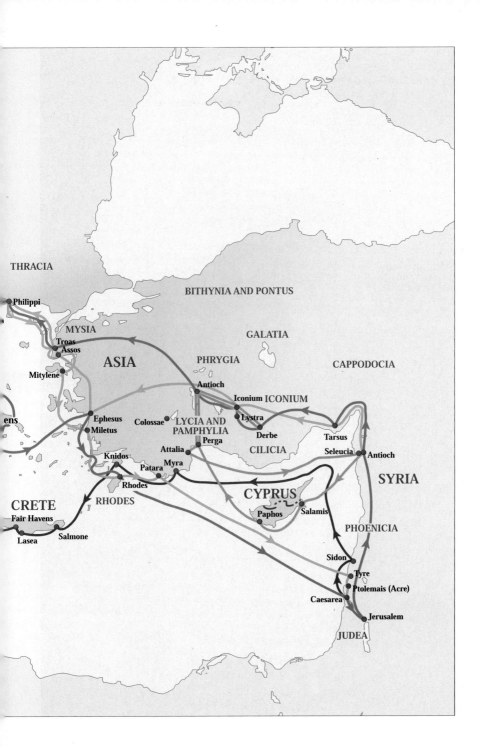

Preface

As with the companion volume, 'A Pilgrim's Guide to the Holy Land', this book aims to provide information in a concise and portable way. It does not pretend to be a comprehensive guide to the countries covered, but rather to concentrate on those areas and sites most likely to excite the interest of the Christian visitor. Its intention is to be a handy reference book, giving sufficient detail to enable the reader to assimilate easily the relevant data about particular locations, whether it is read on a plane or coach, or even in an hotel room! There will be other times for reading more widely and deeply. Probably the vast majority of people who read this book will have previously visited the Holy Land, maybe more than once. They will, therefore, be familiar with the idea of a pilgrimage or holiday with a purpose and the special benefits gained from travelling with a group of like-minded people. 'Fellowship' can be an over-used word, but its original meaning of 'sharing in the Spirit' is particularly apt for those seeking to follow in the steps of St.Paul. After all, his whole missionary enterprise was prompted and promoted by the Holy Spirit and we who seek to trace something of his journeys do so in that same Spirit. No attempt is made in this book to follow the Apostle's travels in any chronological order of the three missionary journeys, as the Christian pilgrim intent on learning something of St.Paul and the places he visited is likely to do so country by country. Our hope is that the information contained in these pages will assist the understanding and, indeed, enjoyment of these Mediterranean locations. We would also offer this book as some small contribution to appreciating more fully the background both to the life and faith of St. Paul himself, and to the thrilling story of the growth and development of the early Church. And along the way, who knows how our own faith and concern for the mission of the contemporary Church may be enhanced as a result of such journeys?

Raymond Goodburn & David Houseley
2001

Ephesus, the colonnaded street

PART 1 From Jerusalem to Rome

After the Resurrection, the first Apostles were charged by the Risen Christ with the responsibility that as well as being witnesses in Jerusalem they should also be witnesses 'to the ends of the earth.' However, the impetus to turn that vision into reality came from a very unlikely source, one Saul of Tarsus. Commissioned on behalf of Judaism to stamp out this new, upstart religion, little did he know that on just such an assignment to Damascus he, Saul, the Christian persecutor, was to undergo a change in life so dramatic that he was in due course to become Paul, the Christian missionary, the prime agent of fulfilling the post-Resurrection vision.

Much of the story of the Acts of the Apostles deals with the exploits of this remarkable man who, in company with others, was to take the Christian Gospel from the heart of Judaism in Jerusalem to the centre of the Roman Empire in Rome itself. Despite hostility, imprisonment, shipwreck, suffering, privation, he single-mindedly adhered to the Damascus Road experience and all that it meant for him as someone appointed to proclaim the Gospel not only to the Jews but also to the Gentiles. From Jerusalem to Rome, from Jew to Gentile, such became the all-embracing mission of the early Church.

There are three main missionary journeys outlined in the Acts. The **first journey** (Acts 13:4-15:4) begins with the selection of Saul and Barnabas for this pioneering work. Beginning in Cyprus, the home of Barnabas, it is during his time here that the author of Acts refers to Saul by his Roman name of Paul, the name by which he is known from this point onwards. Sailing from Paphos, they journey north to Pamphylia and Pisidia, now known as southern and central Turkey. It is while they are in Perga that John Mark, who has travelled this far with them, decides to return to Jerusalem (Acts 13:13), apparently much to the annoyance of Paul (Acts 15:37ff).

In the aftermath of this first journey is the great Council of Acts 15, called together to debate what requirements, if any, should be laid upon Gentiles who become Christians. Once matters have been resolved, envoys led by Paul and Barnabas are appointed to make the Council's decisions known.

This becomes the spring-board for **The second journey** (Acts 15:36-18:22) which, however, begins with Paul and Barnabas parting company over their disagreement about John Mark. Instead, Mark accompanies Barnabas to Cyprus and Silas becomes Paul's new travelling companion. On their travels through Cilicia, Galatia and Phrygia (modern Turkey) Paul and Silas re-visit some of the churches from the first journey, and at Lystra a young man named Timothy becomes another companion. But it is at Troas that the Christian enterprise takes a colossal leap forward. Having received a vision beckoning him to go over into Macedonia, Paul sails from Troas to Macedonia and so the Gospel which has taken root in Asia now spreads over into Europe. Landing in Neapolis, he travels a short distance inland to Philippi, and so begins a journey through Greece which takes him to the capital city of Macedonia, Thessalonika, and from here southwards to Athens, the founder of democracy and the centre of philosophy, literature and art. Nearby Corinth is the next destination, a cosmopolitan and commercial centre, where Paul stays for some considerable time before returning by way of Ephesus to Antioch-on-the-Orontes, from where he set out.

The end of the second missionary journey more or less runs straight into **The third journey,** (Acts 18:23-21:17) so little time does Paul spend in Antioch before setting off again on his travels. He begins in Asia, visiting the churches in Phrygia and Galatia before arriving once more in Ephesus, a journey which must have taken several months. His stay in Ephesus lasts for over two years until a riot by the silversmiths, whose profits appear to have been somewhat eroded by Paul's preaching, signals that it is time to move on. Once more he crosses into Europe from Asia, wanting to strengthen his churches in Macedonia, and spends about three months in Greece, including time in Corinth. Due to a plot by his Jewish enemies, he decides not to return to Jerusalem by sailing directly from Greece to Syria, but makes a detour overland to Philippi and sails from here back to Troas. Choosing to go by land from Troas to Assos rather than sail around the promontory, Paul then takes a boat down the west coast of Turkey arriving in a few days at Miletus, where, having summoned the Ephesian elders, he addresses them and takes an emotional farewell. Sailing south by way of Cos, Rhodes and Patara, Paul and his party transfer to another boat for the journey to Syria, and after landing at Tyre travel to Jerusalem by way of Ptolemais (Acre) and Caesarea.

2

But his arrival in Jerusalem sparks all kinds of trouble, leading ultimately to his arrest and his appeal, as a Roman citizen, to present his case to the Emperor and this, in turn, occasions his final journey, **The journey to Rome.** Imprisoned for some two years in Caesarea, Paul defends himself before two Governors, Felix and Festus, as well as before the King, Agrippa II. Had Paul not appealed to Caesar then he might well have been released, as the charges against him could not be substantiated - such is the advice of Agrippa to Festus. But having made the appeal, to Rome Paul must go.

Under Roman guard, he sails first to Myra (Demre) and then to Crete. Against Paul's advice, the captain determines to press on with the journey in spite of the worsening weather conditions, typical for the winter period. The result is a terrible storm leading to the shipwreck off Malta, vividly described in Acts 27:13-28:10, and where they are then compelled to spend the winter. Eventually, after three months on the island, they are able to set sail once more and by way of Syracuse, Rhegium and Puteoli, Paul finally arrives in Rome, though presumably not in the way he may previously have imagined.

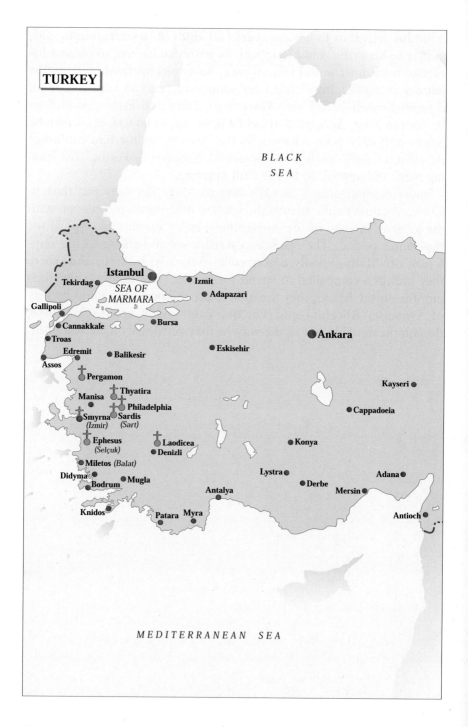

TURKEY

BLACK SEA

Istanbul
Tekirdag
SEA OF MARMARA
Izmit
Adapazari
Gallipoli
Cannakkale
Bursa
Troas
Edremit
Balikesir
Eskisehir
Ankara
Assos
Pergamon
Kayseri
Manisa
Thyatira
Smyrna
(Izmir)
Philadelphia
Sardis
(Sart)
Cappadoeia
Ephesus
(Selçuk)
Laodicea
Denizli
Konya
Miletos (Balat)
Didyma
Bodrum
Mugla
Lystra
Derbe
Adana
Antalya
Mersin
Knidos
Patara
Myra
Antioch

MEDITERRANEAN SEA

St Paul in Turkey

The previous chapter will have illustrated just how important the land of Turkey was in the spread of early Christianity, not only in Asia Minor itself but from there as a springboard into Europe. But alongside Paul we need to mention the name of John, the author of the Book of the Revelation, written from the island of Patmos. Dated in the last decade of the first century during the persecution of Domitian, the most significant part of the Revelation for the pilgrim is the letters to the Seven Churches in Asia Minor, most of which churches, if not all, the pilgrim is likely to visit as part of a tour to Western Turkey. In addition, what also needs to be acknowledged is that between AD 325 and AD 787, Turkey acted as host to seven Ecumenical Councils. The first one, for example, was called by the Emperor Constantine himself and held in the Emperor's palace in Nicea (AD 325). It was charged with the responsibility of defining orthodox Christian belief and as a result produced what is now known as the Nicene Creed. Others dealt with the question of the Person of Christ, 'truly God, truly Man' in one person, particularly the Council of Chalcedon in AD 451. So whilst modern Turkey is secular in government and predominantly Moslem in religion, its Christian past is singularly noteworthy.

A Brief History

Old Testament names such as Noah, whose Ark is believed to have settled on Mount Ararat in Eastern Turkey, and Abraham, whose home was Edessa (modern Urfa), indicate something of the ancient civilisation of Anatolia or Asia Minor, as the region was known until more recently. The earliest signs of human habitation are believed to go back to Neanderthal times, but evidence for the first settled communities is dated about 6000 BC.

The subsequent historical development of Turkey is much too detailed for the scope of a book such as this, but it is important to note particular peoples who created such a rich kaleidoscope of history. The **Persians,** for example, began their dominance of Anatolia in 547 BC when King Croesus was defeated by the Persian, Cyrus the

Great (the same Cyrus who liberated the Jews from Babylon in 539 BC). A major contribution of this period seems to have been the building of an excellent system of roads.

The area remained under the influence of the Persians for some two hundred years until the arrival of Alexander the Great in 334 BC ushered in the **Greek** period. As well as liberating the people of Anatolia, Alexander did much to spread the Greek influence throughout the region, in particular the Greek language and literature. At the same time large new cities were built such as Pergamum and Antioch, with theatres, stadiums and gymnasiums, and most of the ruins which can be seen today stem either from the Greek or Roman periods.

The **Roman** influence began when, in 133 BC, the last King of Pergamum, Attalus III, recognising the increasing power of the Empire in the region, bequeathed his Kingdom to the Romans. From then on began the gradual advance of Rome and the taking over of the various provinces, bringing with it an era of prosperity and political stability. Cities grew both in size and splendour, universities were created, the arts flourished, sport and recreational facilities developed.

During this time thriving Jewish communities established themselves in the cities and it was among these that Christianity found the basis for its rapid expansion throughout the region. As noted in the previous chapter, the agent of this growth was St. Paul, a native of Tarsus in southern Anatolia, who travelled the region and beyond during the years AD 45 to 58.

However, as Christianity grew, so too did opposition and the 2nd and 3rd centuries AD saw periodic outbreaks of persecution against the Christians right across the Empire, the most severe in AD 303 during the time of the Emperor Diocletian. All this changed, though, when **Constantine,** who ruled from AD 324 to 337, converted to Christianity. But as well as embracing Christianity he made another decision which was to have a profound effect on Anatolia. He moved his capital from Rome to Byzantium, which he re-named Constantinople, and the **Byzantine Empire** was born, effectively dividing the Roman Empire into east and west, and while the west diminished in influence so the east flourished. Probably the greatest period of Byzantine rule was during the reign of Justinian (AD 527-565) and one of his most notable achievements was the building of the Church of St.Sophia, dedicated in AD 536, and regarded as the architectural masterpiece of is day.

But from this time onwards the Byzantine influence slowly began to wane (apart from a brief revival in the 9th and 10th centuries) and eventually the centrality of Christianity with it. In AD 654 Arab armies coming from the east brought with them the religion of Islam, which was ultimately to become the religion of the country. Even though the writing was on the wall in 1204 when a Fourth Crusade attacked and looted Constantinople, it was not until the 29th May 1453 that the city finally fell, the last bastion of all that remained from the once mighty Byzantine era.

From then until 1923 it was the **Ottoman Empire** which held the ascendancy. Under Sultan Suleyman (popularly known as Suleyman the Magnificent) it reached its zenith during the period of his rule (1520-1566). Though the title 'Magnificent' was first given to him by Europeans, his own people regarded him primarily as 'Lawgiver', for a significant feature of Ottoman rule was justice for the people. This was an age of major military conquest and expansion, making the Ottoman Empire one of the world's greatest. But as well as being statesman and lawgiver, Suleyman was also credited as a notable patron of the arts and under him the Empire's culture blossomed.

But it was not to last. Though the Empire continued to expand during the early part of the 17th century, the 18th and 19th centuries were a time of steady decline, brought on by pressures from without and conflicts from within. By the end of the First World War during which the Turks sided with the Germans, the Empire fell apart. Yet out of this war and in particular the one successful Turkish military action, that of defending the Gallipoli peninsula, there emerged the man who was to transform the nation - **Mustafa Kemal.** On the 29th October 1923 he was elected the first president of the Turkish Republic and took the name **Ataturk** ('Father of the Turks'). His charismatic and determined leadership launched a process of secularisation and westernisation in government, in religion, in education and in dress which was to lay the foundation of modern Turkey.

But since then there have been many ups-and-downs, especially in trying to find political stability and, indeed, between 1960 and the present day there have been no less than three coups! Whilst currently the government is looking for EU membership, there are those who think that the country should look east rather than west for its political and economic partners. In addition, the change since 1923 from a predominantly rural nation to an urban one has put enormous strains on the cities, not least the problems caused by the influx of large numbers of migrants into them. Nor can the increase in fundamentalism be overlooked. The Kurdish question, too, is one which as yet remains unresolved, as also is the issue of northern Cyprus with its consequent stand-off between Greece and Turkey.

But none of this should deter the would-be pilgrim from visiting the country and exploring the sites associated with the early growth and development of Christianity in the region. After all, no country the Christian pilgrim visits is going to be without its problems. Those seeking to discover the background both to the mission of the early Church and to the very rich past and present of Turkey, will find that they do so among friendly and hospitable hosts.

Pergamum

Western Turkey

Beginning on the north-western coast of Turkey and progressing steadily south down the Aegean coast to the Mediterranean, **Alexandria Troas** is the starting point for this particular journey. Visited twice by St. Paul, it was on the second missionary journey that he here heard the call to take his preaching across the Aegean and into Macedonia (Greece). On the third journey, returning from Macedonia, he stayed in Troas for a week. On this occasion, while Paul was speaking at great length, a young man named Eutychus, who was sitting in a window, fell asleep and tumbled out of the window, landing three floors below. However, when Paul went down to examine him, he was found not to have come to any great harm (Acts 20:5-12).

Once a major port, Troas was founded by one of the generals of Alexander the Great. The site today is much neglected, though the walls of its impressive baths are still on view. Much of its stonework was transferred from here to help with the building of the new capital, Constantinople.

While in this region, it is possible to visit **Troy**, the city of Homer's "Iliad". The stories relating to Achilles, to Helen, to the wooden horse, have all fired the imagination. Indeed there have been those who considered that ancient Troy might be little more than a creation of Homer's own imagination, for by the 6th century AD Troy had been abandoned, its harbour had silted up, and all physical traces had disappeared. All that remained was a hill.

Then, in the 1870's a German named Heinrich Schliemann began a series of excavations to unearth Homer's Troy, and in the process discovered not just one site for the city, but nine, the oldest dating back to about 3600 BC. But still the debate about Troy has continued and in particular, whether the Trojan War (c.1250 BC) took place as told by Homer.

The entrace to the site is dominated by a modern replica of the famous Wooden Horse, an evocative reminder of the stirring events it is believed to represent. The site itself is something of a mish-mash of the various cities of Troy. The visitor can see, among other things, the particularly impressive, though not extensive, walls of Troy VI, the foundations of a bastion, the ruins of the Temple of Athena, the chariot ramp, as well as other remains dating back to the time of the Romans.

Another possible excursion, though again not connected with St. Paul, is to **Gallipoli,** which can be reached either by road from Istanbul or by ferry across the Dardanelles from Cannakkale. This was the scene of of one of the bloodiest battles of the Great War as British Empire and French forces took the only route for them, by sea through the Dardanelles, in an attempt to re-supply the Russians on the eastern front. But the Turkish army, Germany's ally, stood in the way and after colossal loss of life on both sides, the allies retreated in January 1916. Visits can be made to nearby **Anzac Cove,** to see the graves of Australian and New Zealand troops and to the military museum.

Returning then to St. Paul: on his third journey Paul travelled overland from here to **Assos** on the other side of the peninsula. After meeting up with his friends who had undertaken the journey by boat, they then set sail south towards Miletus.

The surrounding area is delightfully rural, giving the impression of a traditional way of life that has changed very little for centuries. As you approach Assos the outline of the acropolis can be seen in the distance. A walk up through the village below leads to the top of the hill and the acropolis itself. In its heyday Assos was a centre of learning and teaching, for Aristotle, Plato's most famous pupil, lived and taught here for some three years. The citadel is surrounded by walls which stretch for about 2 miles and in places are as high as 46 feet, and set within the citadel is the 6th century BC Temple of Athena. All that remains today is the platform of the acropolis and a number of Doric columns. But to stand among the ruins and soak up the wonderful view across the Aegean and the Gulf of Edremit amply repays the uphill walk. While here there is an opportunity to buy samples of local lace-making and enjoy some refreshment at a most welcoming little restaurant.

Ephesus

Visited by St. Paul towards the end of his second journey and again on his third, when he stayed here for over two years, Ephesus stands unrivalled among the sites of Turkey. At the height of its splendour it

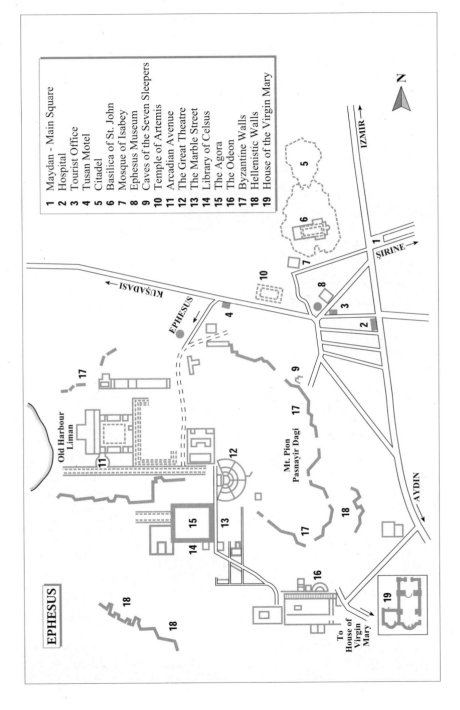

EPHESUS

1 Maydan - Main Square
2 Hospital
3 Tourist Office
4 Tusan Motel
5 Citadel
6 Basilica of St. John
7 Mosque of Isabey
8 Ephesus Museum
9 Caves of the Seven Sleepers
10 Temple of Artemis
11 Arcadian Avenue
12 The Great Theatre
13 The Marble Street
14 Library of Celsus
15 The Agora
16 The Odeon
17 Byzantine Walls
18 Hellenistic Walls
19 House of the Virgin Mary

N

IZMIR →

ŞIRINE →

← KUŞADASI

EPHESUS →

Old Harbour
Liman

Mt. Pion
Pasnayir Dagi

AYDIN →

To
House of
Virgin
Mary

The theatre at Ephesus

was the foremost city of Asia, due to two main features. The first was the harbour, making Ephesus a natural centre for trade throughout the Mediterranean region, so establishing its commercial and banking significance. The second was the Temple of Artemis/Diana, one of the Seven Wonders of the Ancient World, to which visitors flocked from all over, bringing their gifts for the goddess, a further contributory factor to the wealth and pre-eminence of the city. But the constant threat to its prosperity was the silting up of the harbour and by the 6th century AD this had happened to such a degree that the city was abandoned and a new one created nearby - modern Selçuk. Nowadays the sea is some 5 miles away from Ephesus.

Though originally a classical Greek city, most of what is to be seen now dates from the Roman period. There is much to be said for beginning a tour of the site from the eastern entrance, so allowing a gradual build-up of impact as you eventually approach its most spectacular features.

From the east the route takes you past, among other things, the East Gymnasium, the Odeon, used more as a meeting place than for concerts, the State Agora, the Temple of Domitian, dated to the 1st century AD and one of four Temples, and the Fountain of Trajan. As the colonnaded road begins to drop downhill there is a splendid view down to the Library of Celsus at the bottom. But first, notice the Temple of Hadrian on the right, partially restored and particularly attractive. Opposite here is a recently excavated residential area, where the rich and the powerful lived in their luxurious mansions. Nearby, too, are the public toilets (Not the modern ones!). Then, as the road turns to the right, it is the magnificent Library of Celsus which claims the attention. A strikingly elegant building, the morning light best helps to highlight its features. Built by Julius Aquila in memory of his father Celsus, whose sarcophagus is in a tomb under the Library, it presents a most impressive facade of marble adorned with carvings and statues. With a reading room set on three levels, it possessed one of the largest collections of books at that time.

Continuing from the Library along the Marble Road in the direction of the harbour brings you to the Theatre which, of all the buildings in Ephesus, is the best-known for the Christian pilgrim. This is where, during Paul's two year stay in the city, a group of silversmiths led by Demetrius caused something of a riot in protest at the preaching of Paul and his companions. As makers of images of Diana, the silversmiths clearly saw that conversions to Christianity were a threat to their work and livelihood. Paul's colleagues, Gaius and Aristarchus, were dragged into the theatre before the mob, but he himself was restrained from joining them by some of his followers and local officials. Once the trouble had subsided Paul very soon left Ephesus for Macedonia.

Estimated to hold 24,000 people and the largest in Turkey, the theatre was originally of Greek design but then transformed by the Romans. If you can summon up the energy it is well worth the climb to the top seats for a fine view over the city and especially the harbour area. Also, should there be someone in the group with a good speaking voice or even if a group wants to sing, it is a splendid place for experiencing the marvellous acoustic of such buildings.

Leaving the theatre and following the marble-paved and colonnaded road in the harbour direction, brings you to the point where the coach will pick you up if you have begun your visit to Ephesus from the eastern end. But before moving on from the site there is one more visit which may be made, and that is to the Church of St. Mary, a short walk not far from the parking area. A long, narrow building and sometimes described as 'the double church', it may not even have been a church in the first instance. No one seems quite sure about its original usage, maybe a bank and market, but once it was converted into a church it was dedicated to the Virgin Mary and is said to be the first church ever dedicated to her. It was here in AD 431 that the Third Ecumenical Council met.

For the Christian pilgrim there are two further possible visits in the vicinity. One is to the House of the Virgin Mary, set in the forested hills near Ephesus. There is a tradition which says that Mary came here with St. John and this is where she spent the last years of her life, though there is another tradition that the site of her death is on Mt. Zion in Jerusalem. Whatever the pros and cons, the house has become an important pilgrimage centre, especially on 15th August to celebrate the Feast of the Assumption.

The other worthwhile visit is to the Basilica of St. John, situated towards the foot of the hill on which stands the dominating fortress of Selcuçk. Built in the 6th century by the Emperor Justinian and now partly reconstructed, it is said to be the burial place of St. John, the spot marked by a raised marble slab. The original church was in the shape of a cross, crowned with six domes and on the site there is a representation of how it probably looked.

Miletus

If from this vantage point you look towards the main site of Ephesus, you will see below you in a field a single, solitary column, all that remains of the once-wondrous Temple of Artemis. First built in the 7th century BC and then replaced in the 6th, it was rebuilt again in the 4th century after having been burned down. A massive structure, some 378ft long and 181ft wide, it was constructed predominantly of marble with a wooden roof and surrounded by 129 columns. In nearby Selçuk, the Archaeological Museum contains two marble statues of Artemis, as well as statues, frescoes, mosaics and coins from Ephesus and deserves a visit.

Some distance inland from Ephesus is all that remains of Colossae, once a major city and famous for the dark red wool called *'colossinum'*. Destroyed by an earthquake in AD 60, as were Laodicea and Hierapolis, there is very little to be seen today. Paul did not himself visit the city (Col. 1:4), though it had been founded by an assistant of his, Epaphras, who appears to have hailed from the city. It was from Epaphras and Onesimus, a runaway slave from Colossae, that Paul heard about the church there. Today the site is unexcavated and when Christian groups visit Colossae it is often linked with visits to nearby Laodicea and Hierapolis (both mentioned in Col. 4:13). A short climb up the hill of Colossae gives a good view of surrounding rural Turkey.

Continuing the journey south along the coastal route from Ephesus will bring you to **Miletus,** which Paul visited towards the end of his third missionary journey (Acts 20:15-38). From here he took his emotional farewell of the Ephesian elders before hurrying off to reach Jerusalem in time for Pentecost.

Settlement began here about 1500 BC and in the Greek period it developed as a major Ionian port at the mouth of the Meander River. Though destroyed by the Persian invasion of 494 BC it was quickly re-built and in Roman times re-established much of its former prominence. But a great deal of Miletus's fame was based not only on commerce but also on philosophy, being the birthplace of notable philosophers and sages such as Thales, Anaximander and Anaximines.

On arrival by coach at Miletus the first thing that strikes you is the Theatre, set in a hillside and facing the parking area. Of all the ruins here it is by far the most grand and, indeed, best preserved. Reconstructed by the Romans it could seat at least 15,000 people. A walk over the hill from the theatre brings you to the city centre, where you will find a council chamber, nymphaeum, a 2nd century BC stadium, three market places, a synagogue, a 5th century AD church and a mosque. It is also still possible to find the two lions which guarded the entrance to the harbour. But after the theatre, the most well preserved of all the buildings is the Baths of Faustina dedicated to Faustina, the wife of Marcus Aurelius.

Southern Turkey

Journeying further to the south towards the Mediterranean brings us to **Knidos** (Cnidus). On his final voyage to Rome, the captain of Paul's ship intended to land at Cnidus but the severity of the winds made this impossible (Acts 27:7), so the only claim to Pauline fame was as a landfall rather than a place visited by him. Founded in the 4th century BC and once a flourishing city renowned as a centre of art, many of the finds from here are on display in the British Museum. A stepped street, houses, a theatre, and the foundations of the circular temple of Aphrodite can be seen. Though possible to reach by land, it is most accessible by means of a boat-trip.

Following the coastline around towards the east, the next significant place associated with Paul is **Patara.** On the way to Jerusalem from Miletus towards the end of his third missionary journey, Paul called in here (Acts 21:1). They changed to another ship, possibly a larger one, for the final, longer stage of their journey. But Patara was also the birthplace of Nicholas (c.AD 300), who, as well as becoming the first Bishop of Myra, was also at a later stage to be popularly known as St. Nicholas (*ie* as Santa Claus).

Once a major port at the mouth of the Xanthus River, making it the principal port of Lycia, Patara suffered a similar fate to that of Ephesus, namely, the silting up of its harbour. Alexander the Great and Brutus were both associated with its famous past. Most of the ruins date from Patara's greatest days of the Roman period - the triple-arched gate (c.AD 100), the theatre, which is partially covered by the invading sands, the granary of Hadrian, temples, baths and a Christian basilica.Whilst it can no longer boast about its harbour, it most certainly can about its magnificent sandy beach.

Continuing eastwards we arrive in **Demre** (Kale), site of ancient Myra and Bishopric of St. Nicholas. On his journey to Rome from Caesarea, Paul, along with other prisoners plus some of his friends, stopped off at this important port and changed ships (Acts 27:5-6).

The main point of interest in Demre itself is the St. Nicholas Church, dating back originally to the 5th century. Used earlier this century as a substitute for a mosque, the development of tourism enhanced the potential of the church, and, after much restoration, it was opened in 1981 as a shrine and museum to St. Nicholas. Indeed, there are those who associate the origins of Santa Claus with this place in Turkey rather than with snowy locations somewhat further north! The site of ancient **Myra** is about one mile from the town on the northern outskirts and is noted for two sets of Lycian tombs hewn out of the cliffs as well as a huge Roman theatre. Lycian inscriptions and carvings can be seen.

Moving on from here we reach **Antalya,** possibly Turkey's most beautiful city set in the most beautiful surroundings, and currently the thriving centre of this vastly popular tourist area, an excellent base for visiting either holiday or ancient locations. It was from Antalya (Attalia), then in the region of Pamphylia, that Paul sailed on his way back to Antioch-on-the-Orontes (Acts 14:24-26) at the completion of his first missionary journey.

The town was founded by Attalus II, King of Pergamum, in the 2nd century BC, though an original settlement here is believed to go back to at least 1000 BC. Particularly impressive among the remains on view is Hadrian's Gate, a triple-arched marble gate to commemorate the Emperor's visit to the city in AD 130. Also to be seen are city walls and ramparts, built originally by the Greeks but later restored by the Romans and Selçuks. The Yivlie Minare (the 'fluted minaret') is the distinctive symbol of Antalya and the most memorable of all the splendid minarets you are likely to see during a visit to Turkey. It was once part of a mosque complex built by the Selçuks in the 13th century and is a fine example of Selçuk craftsmanship. Notice, too, the Hidirlik Tower, possibly once a lighthouse and said to contain the tomb of a 2nd century Roman consul.

But before leaving Antalya, pay a visit to the Archaeological Museum, displaying exhibits from the Stone Age through to a 6th century AD relief of the Archangel Gabriel. Greek and Roman sculptures abound, and there is a sarcophagus reputed to hold the remains of St. Nicholas of Myra himself.

Almost next door to Antalya is **Perge,** visited by Paul along with Barnabas and John Mark on the first missionary journey (Acts 13:13; 14:25) and, of course, the place where Mark parted company with Paul. Although not as vast as Ephesus and Pergamum, the site of Perge is still particularly impressive. In Hellenistic times it was the principal city of Pamphylia, but it was largely under the Romans that it reached its greatest prosperity. Before entering the impressive double gates to the city, the visitor will first see the magnificent theatre and horse-shoe shaped stadium, one of the best preserved in the ancient world. A climb to the top of the theatre furnishes a wonderful view over the city. Inside the city walls are baths, a colonnaded street and, next to the agora are the remains of a Byzantine basilica. Further into the city are the foundations of the cathedral.

Though not all Christian pilgrims following the steps of St. Paul will travel much further east along the Mediterranean coast than this, there will be some who do, especially those who want to visit the birthplace of the Apostle, **Tarsus** itself. Although also associated with the first meeting between Mark Antony and Cleopatra, Tarsus, however, is identified in religious history with Paul himself. Here Paul was born a Jew of the tribe of Benjamin, in due course inheriting Roman citizenship and its rights from his father, from whom he probably developed his trade as a tentmaker. It was to Tarsus that Barnabas later came to recruit Paul, or Saul as he then was, to share the Christian work in Antioch-on-the-Orontes (Acts 11:25).

Though Tarsus itself has a rich history, once being a significant Cilician trading port situated on a lagoon, there is little to be observed today in the way of remains which testify to its antiquity, much of which is buried beneath the modern town. Any references to 'St. Paul's Gate', 'St. Paul's Well', or even 'St. Paul's House' should not be taken too seriously! But for pilgrims who do venture this far, maybe it will be enough just to have visited the location of Paul's birth.

Before leaving this southern, Mediterranean coast of Turkey, mention ought to be made of one more Pauline location, even further east and close to the border with Syria - **Antioch-on-the-Orontes.** Indeed, so close is it to the Syrian border, that Christian pilgrims are much more likely to visit Antioch from Syria rather than from Turkey itself. Set in a delightfully fertile plain and surrounded by hills, Antioch was once the prosperous and flamboyant capital of the Seleucids, whose kings were noted for their indulgent lifestyles. Founded originally by one of the generals of Alexander the Great, the city flourished during this Hellenistc period, becoming the most significant city in the region, boasting many impressive buildings. It prospered even further under the Romans when it became capital of the province of Syria, establishing itself as a centre of commerce and culture, becoming the third city of the Empire after Rome and Alexandria.

The best way of seeing the coast of south west Turkey is by gulet

This, then, was the city which served as a base for the work of Peter, Paul and Barnabas. A grotto east of the city and known as the Church of St. Peter, is said to be where Peter first preached and began to consolidate the Christian community in the city. As mentioned previously, it was from here that Barnabas went to Tarsus to bring Paul back with him to act as a helper with the Christian mission in Antioch and it was from here, too, that they set out on their first missionary journey (Acts 13:1-3). It should also be mentioned that it was in Antioch that the followers of Jesus were first called 'Christians' (Acts 11:26).

Central Turkey

This is an area which embraces the remaining sites associated with St. Paul, as well as the unique region of Cappadocia with its amazing landscape and underground cities, a region of compelling allure. But first, let us complete our survey of Paul in Turkey.

Derbe and **Lystra** are both mentioned during the first missionary journey when Paul and Barnabas, on learning of a plot to stone them in Iconium, fled here (Acts 14:1-23). However, having healed a crippled man in Lystra, Paul's opponents from Antioch in Pisidia and Iconium so influenced the crowds in Lystra, that they stoned him and dragged him out of the city, thinking that he was dead (Acts 14:19-20). Paul and Barnabas then moved on to Derbe where they appear to have received a much more favourable reception and made many converts (Acts 14:21). Today little remains of these sites.

Iconium (Konya), however, is a different matter. In spite of the opposition they met here, Paul and Barnabas do seem to have been reasonably successful, making many converts (Acts 14:1) and on the strength of that stayed for some time. Nowadays the city is a centre for both Christian and Moslem pilgrims.

It has a long history, created by Hittites, Phyrgians, Lydians, Persians, Greeks and then Romans. But it was during its time as the capital of the Selçuk Empire (1071-1308) that the city experienced a significant cultural renaissance. The beauty of its Selçuk architecture in such buildings as the Alâeddin Mosque (with its Roman columns) the Karatay Medresesi (a museum of Selçuk and Ottoman ceramics set in a 13th-century Selçuk theological seminary), and, of course, the Mevlana Museum, which houses the tomb of Mevlana Celaleddin Rumi, founder of the famous 'Whirling Dervishes'. The museum also contains traditional Dervish garments, prayer carpets, and the earliest edition of Mevlana's great poetical and mystical work, The *Mesnevi*. Accompanied by a reed flute, the whirling of the dancers expresses their search for a mystical union with God.

Antioch-of-Pisidia (Yalvaç) brings us to the final place associated with the travels and preaching of St. Paul in Asia Minor. As seen above, his activities here during the first missionary journey as well as creating converts also created dissent (Acts 13:14-52). Originally a Phrygian settlement, the town was founded between 300 and 280 BC and for a long time was the main town of Pisidia. Set on a hillside, a few scattered ruins mark the site. There are the remains of an arched entrance, a temple, a church and basilica, as well as an aqueduct. The local museum at Yalvaç houses some of the findings from the site.

This, then, completes our travels with St. Paul through Turkey. We can only marvel at the faith and fortitude of a man whose life was so driven by his experience on the road to Damascus and his missionary zeal, that out of the cradle of Asia Minor there matured a Christian Church whose influence was to become world-wide.

Cappadocia

It can be said without fear of contradiction that there is no place on earth quite like Cappadocia. The unique landscape, created by nature over millions of years, could almost be something out of a fairy-tale. The origin of this amazing topography is due to volcanic eruption all that time ago, which covered the region with a thick layer of lava and volcanic ash called tuff. This, in turn, when worked upon by the elements, created a fantastic landscape of valleys along with rocky outcrops sculptured into the most amazing shapes. These outcrops have become known as 'fairy chimneys'. The early inhabitants of the region quickly discovered that the stone is soft until it comes into contact with the air and with this knowledge they were able to carve out their homes from the rock. Much later still, Christians fleeing from Roman and subsequently Arab persecution, created their underground cities, monasteries and churches.

Whilst many Christian pilgrims to Turkey will initially concentrate on Western Turkey, both to explore the Pauline sites and those associated with the Seven Churches, hopefully, if Cappadocia is not part of that initial programme, they will want to return and discover this unique region. Though there is no evidence that St. Paul visited what is today called 'Cappadocia', it has to be remembered that originally the Hellenistic Kingdom and subsequent Roman province of Cappadocia was much more extensive and would certainly have included Iconium (Konya). Once Christianity took root, the region developed into a stronghold of Christian monasticism, with Basil the Great in the 4th century as its dominant figure. As Bishop of Caesarea (now Kayseri) he formulated the monastic rules which were the basis of the monastic communities that established themselves in the area.

As there is much more to be seen than the normal tour itinerary will accommodate, we will concentrate on particular highlights. The capital of the region and an ideal base from which to explore is **Nevşehir** (meaning 'new town'). Though there is not a great deal of antiquity here, as the name of the town implies, it is worth climbing up to the ruined Selçuk castle which affords a splendid viewing point for the area around. Also take time to visit the Damad Ibrahim Paşa Mosque, named after the man who did so much to introduce European art and culture into Turkey.

Travelling south from Nevşehir we come first to **Kaymakli** and then **Derinkuyu,** two of the six underground cities so far discovered in the region, though at the time of writing only three are available for viewing. So extensive are these cities that excavations are by no means complete. Several storeys in depth, they were used by Christians seeking to escape from persecution and were capable of accommodating thousands of people, possibly as many as 20,000. However, the discovery of Roman tombs and what may be a Hittite grain mill, suggests that these cities are considerably older. There are churches, living quarters, dining areas, storage rooms and even tombs, all linked by underground tunnels, some as long as six miles, fresh air being supplied by an efficient system of vertical air shafts. The depth of these air shafts, some more than 100 metres, gives an idea of the vast scale of these cities, built storey on storey, only some of which are open to the public. The tunnels themselves even contained huge blocking stones by which they could be sealed off quickly in the event of invasion. Marvels of construction, one can only guess at the time-span required to create these labyrynthine cities, but it must have been centuries.

Travelling eastwards from Nevşehir brings us to the Rock of Üçhisar. One of a number of rock cities in the area it provides an example of how cave dwellings were carved out of the rockface. The climb to the top is recommended for the panoramic view it provides of the Göreme Valley. A few miles further east we arrive at **Göreme** itself and to the Göreme Valley Museum, an open-air museum of numerous rock-cut churches dating back to the 10th and 11th centuries, many with beautifully preserved frecoes. This is the largest monastic complex in the area, but even then it represents only a fraction of the 3,500 or so such churches in Cappadocia. Many of them have been sculptured in such a way as to create arches, pillars, domes,

ABOVE: *Fairy chimneys in Cappadocia*
BELOW: *Pergamum*

as in an ordinary church, but the main difference being that there are no windows. The significance of the paintings is that they portray in art-form the history, beliefs and customs of the people who designed them. Some depict New Testament scenes, others lives of the saints (including St. George with his dragon), along with those whose stories are unfamiliar to us.

Not far from Göreme, in a north-easterly direction, is **Zelve,** another canyon full of rock churches and in places dense with fairy chimneys. Also, if opportunity permits, do try to visit the **Ihlara Valley,** situated south-westerly from Nevşehir. With its steep-sided, red cliffs and fertile green valley, it provides the most dramatic and picturesque of all the settings for the many rock churches, some of which probably date back to the 6th century. Many of these, too, are decorated with excellent frescoes. Needless to say, there are countless rock houses as well.

Though it seems trite to say it, Cappadocia has to be seen to be believed. With its incredible and surrealistic landscape, its underground cities, monasteries, rock churches and paintings, there really is nowhere quite like it and a visit here cannot be anything less than memorable.

The Seven Churches

Whatever else they do, Christian pilgrims visiting Western Turkey will want to trace not just the steps of St. Paul but also the sites of the Seven Churches addressed by the author of the Book of the Revelation. But before we inspect these locations some background on the book may help to set the scene.

So obscure is the language and imagery of the Book of The Revelation, that many Christians are inclined to give up the unequal struggle and leave it to those for whom it has become a happy hunting-ground of exotic ideas about the future and, indeed, the present. The cause of the book is not helped by those of its exponents who seek to stamp a literalism on its imagery and poetry that they were never meant to bear. Much of the language of Revelation is that of visionary poetry and any attempt to force a literal interpretation on it is to do violence to what the author intended. But to those who are prepared to work with the poetry and symbolism, and, therefore, grapple with the ideas they represent, then the book comes across as a powerful and original work about Jesus Christ as the final and authoritative revelation of God's purposes for history.

Who was the author? A 2nd century AD tradition suggests that the author of the Revelation is the same as that of the gospel and letters of John. Yet, although there may be certain hints of the language of the fourth gospel, so very different is the style and content of the Revelation, that it is extremely difficult to ascribe authorship to the same person. Maybe the most we can say from the evidence available is that the author was a Jewish Christian whose name was John, writing towards the end of the first century, with some knowledge of the ideas in John's gospel, and who was regarded by some churches in Asia Minor as being a person of authority. What is more, he was writing against a background of Christian persecution during the time of Domition. He himself seems to have suffered for his faith and was writing from exile on the island of Patmos, though the degree of his personal suffering is not known.

A letter to Ephesus (Revelation 2:1-7)

Taking the letters in the order in which they appear in the Book of the Revelation, we begin with that to the church in Ephesus. We have already noted that Ephesus was the most significant port in Asia Minor and its most prosperous city, so it is entirely appropriate that the first letter should be to the Christian community here. Each letter has a message specifically addressed to the circumstances of each church and contained within the message is a word of warning relating to that particular situation. The church in Ephesus is praised for the way in which it has withstood heresy from within and persecution from without, but is criticised for losing its early love. Yet as so often in these letters, the negative is followed by a positive word of encouragement (v.7). In terms of Ephesus as an archaeological site, this has been covered previously in pages 10-15.

A letter to Smyrna (Revelation 2:8-11)

Directly north from Ephesus the courier responsible for delivering these letters would have come to Smyrna (modern Izmir). This letter is particularly noteworthy in that it contains no element of blame. The Christians in Smyrna are clearly a struggling community, rich only in their faith, and persecuted by the Jewish community. The warning to the Christians is to remain faithful till death. It is interesting to observe that of all the seven cities, Smyrna is the only one where the church has survived down the centuries. Among several churches in present-day Izmir, Turkey's third largest city, are the Anglican Church of St. John and the Catholic Cathedral of St. John the Evangelist, as well as the Catholic Church of St. Polycarp. In addition, the presence of a large number of synagogues indicates the strength of the Jewish community.

With a foundation going back to pre-history, which includes Hittite remains, ancient Smyrna eventually developed into a prosperous and beautiful city, due mainly to the influence of Alexander the Great in the 4th century BC, who re-sited the city, and later to the Romans. The first Christian congregation would have been drawn from the Jewish community, this in itself being a prime motive for the subsequent persecution. However, by the early part of the 2nd century AD there was clearly a sizeable enough Christian community to support a bishop, the most famous of all being Polycarp, the fourth bishop from

AD 115 to 156 and one of the first Christian martyrs. Arrested and tried by the Roman Governor, Statius Quadratus, Polycarp refused to compromise his allegiance to Christ by acknowledging the sovereignty of the Emperor: 'For eighty and six years I have served Jesus Christ and he has done me no wrong. How can I blaspheme my King?' For his unyielding devotion he was burned at the stake.

Unfortunately, during the evacuation of Greek troops from the region in 1922, a huge, three day fire destroyed much which reflected the history of Izmir. However, not far from the bazaar is one of the most notable remains, the Roman Agora (market place). Rebuilt by Marcus Aurelius after the devastating earthquake of AD 178, two rows of colonnades can still be seen, along with statues to Demeter, Poseidon and Artemis. Overlooking the agora is Kadifekale, the Velvet Castle, perched on Mount Pagus and, according to the legend, it was here that Alexander the Great was told in a dream to re-site the city and its inhabitants. If there is time, the walk to the top provides wonderful views over the city and bay.

A letter to Pergamum (Revelation 2:12-17)

Although most visitors to Western Turkey will highlight the magnificence of Ephesus, even so Pergamum was, and still is, one of the most impressive Classical sites in Turkey. Described by John as the place 'where Satan has his throne', this may be a reference to the temple of Zeus, with its immense altar, or to the power of Rome as embodied in the person of the Roman Governor, who made the city his principal residence. We cannot be sure.

Clearly there had been some local persecution of Christians, yet they had remained faithful. But the real danger to the Christian community seems to have come from the Nicolaitans, also referred to in the letter to Ephesus. Though nothing is known about this group they were regarded by John as a heretical element within the church and intent on threatening the faithful with compromise of religious and ethical standards. To those who stay constant John promises 'manna'. Just as this manna was the supernatural food which sustained the people of Israel in the wilderness, so it will be the food of the chosen in heaven. The reference to the reward of the white stones is extremely obscure but suggests either acquittal or victory.

The site of Pergamum towers over the town of Bergama, famous for its rugs and while in the area you may have chance to visit a factory

Hierapolis

where they are made and even buy the finished product. But be warned - they are hand-made and therefore not cheap. However, if you are more interested in ruins than rugs, then Pergamum itself will enthral you.

It was in the last two centuries BC that Pergamum reached the height of its splendour. During the Greek period it became a principal centre of commerce, culture and medicine and in due course developed into the capital of the Roman Empire in Asia Minor. From Bergama you drive past the **Lower Agora** up to Pergamum's famed **Acropolis**, more than 1,000 feet above the valley below. Once on top you can see the **Upper Agora** and nearby, somewhat higher up, are the remains of the **Altar of Zeus**, of which only the foundations are visible today. The reconstructed altar can be seen in the Pergamum Museum in Berlin. Most spectacular of all is the **Theatre**, with its 80 rows set into the hillside and with a capacity of 10,000 spectators. If you were seated on the top rows you would need a good head for heights! Mind you, as well as a splendid view of the stage you also had an impressive view of the surrounding countryside. Above the theatre and set on the highest level of the acropolis is the imposing Temple of Trajan, on which there has been a good deal of restoration. Adjacent to this is the famous **Library**, said to contain 200,000 volumes, and making it one of the most famous of libraries, a rival even to that of Alexandria, until, that is, Antony gave it to Cleopatra. Alongside the Library is the **Temple of Athena**. In addition to all this are the remains of Palaces and Barracks.

Normal citizens lived further down the hillside and here, as well as the Lower Agora, is the **Temple of Demeter**, along with the upper and middle **Gymnasium**, where young men and adolescents trained and studied. In this area, too, are the remains of shops and houses.

But before leaving the area a visit to nearby **Asclepion** is much recommended. Dedicated to Asclepios, the god of Medicine, this was a kind of health spa in which, for example, an over-wrought businessman, politician or whoever, could come to be 'de-stressed'. Such a person would be led down the colonnaded Sacred Way and offered a choice of facilities to aid the healing process. On offer was psychotherapy, a library with good books, a theatre, and the opportunity for a dip in the sacred waters, which were thought to be a significant part of the healing process.

A letter to Thyatira (Revelation 2:18-29)

Apart from here there is only one other mention of Thyatira in the New Testament and that is during Paul's second missionary journey, when he visited Philippi in Macedonia and there met Lydia, a woman who was selling expensive purple cloth (Acts 16:14). As with the letter to Pergamum, John begins by praising the record of the Christians in Thyatira, but like Pergamum, they are threatened from within. The strong language of the letter warns the congregation that they are in serious danger of being led astray by a heretical group who were wanting to lead them into pagan ways. But as with the other letters this one ends with a promise that those who stand firm against the heresy and who are victorious will share in the sovereignty of Christ.

There is nothing specially impressive about Thyatira's history, though in Hellenistic times it was a garrison of considerable importance for Greek soldiers. Subsequently, when it became part of Rome, industry and commerce seem to have been the main features, with a particular emphasis on making the royal purple cloth. Trade guilds were also very strong. What remains of the ancient town is to be found in the centre of the modern Akhisar. There is part of a colonnaded street, a temple, and walls of a church.

A letter to Sardis (Revelation 3:1-6)

Once the capital of the Lydian kingdom, Sardis was a centre of wealth and influence especially during the reign of Croesus, the last of its kings (560 to 546 BC). A hub of commercial life in the western Mediterranean, much of its wealth was in gold washed down from the mountain by the River Pactolus. Whilst its importance remained undiminished well into the first century BC, an earthquake in AD 17 destroyed most of the city. Though it was rebuilt by the Emperor Tiberius and was to become a centre of Christianity and an eminent bishopric, it never fully regained its previous glory.

Maybe John, in writing his letter to Sardis, was drawing a parallel between the waning influence of the city and the declining enthusiasm of the Christian community. The church is living on its past reputation and rather than being alive it is now dead. Yet, there is still a nucleus who have remained faithful and they will wear the white robes of those who will be admitted to heaven. This, too, is the promise held out to the rest of the Christian community if they wake up and once more begin to live faithfully the way of Christ.

To the modern visitor, one of the most immediately obvious and, indeed, impressive features of the site is the Roman gymnasium and baths dating back to the 2nd century AD. Situated just off the main road, what is seen today is a major reconstruction of this complex. The magnificent entrance to the gymnasium is through columns decorated with the heads of gods. Adjacent to here are the reconstructed remains of a huge synagogue, testifying to the size and influence of the Jewish community. Notice the colourful floor mosaics made from small pieces of marble. Alongside the synagogue is a row of shops, with varying trades identified.

Whilst many tour itineraries may not have time for further exploration, there is, however, more to be seen on the opposite side of the road. The House of Bronzes takes its name from the many pieces of bronze found here, and given their religious character it is possible this may have been the residence of the Bishop of Sardis. But if the gymnasium-bath complex is the most immediately impressive site to the visitor, the Temple of Artemis is undoubtedly its most spectacular. Vast in size it measures approximately 329ft by 165ft and particularly splendid are its two remaining beautiful *Ionic* capitals. Few visitors will have time, or maybe even energy, for the walk up to the acropolis, but a magnificent panoramic view is the reward for those who make the effort.

A Letter to Philadelphia (Revelation 3:7-13)

On reading this particular letter it is instantly noticeable that there is no real note of criticism directed at this particular Christian congregation. The whole tone of the message has a much more gentle character. The church appears to be one of the least distinguished, with little power. Such criticism as it does contain is directed again, as at Sardis, to the members of Satan's synagogue. The Christians are reminded that they have an immense missionary task before them and are promised that for their constancy and endurance they will be pillars in God's temple, in other words, their ultimate salvation is guaranteed.

Philadelphia was founded by Attalus II in the 2nd century BC. The town took its name from the fact that Attalus was called *philadelphus* 'loyal brother', by Eumenes, his brother, who was King of Pergamum before him. Like most towns in the vicinity, Philadelphia suffered from major earthquakes, especially during the reign of Tiberius (AD 14-37), one of the most severe being in AD 17. Little of note is left from the ancient town, though the remaining massive pillars of the church of St. John reflect its Christian past.

Laodicea

A Letter to Laodicea (Revelation 3:14–22)

Whereas the church at Philadelphia was the recipient of unstinting praise, so the church at Laodicea received unmitigated criticism. Not far from either Colossae or Hierapolis, Laodicea was famed for its wealth, its textile trade, and its medical school. But such was the church's compromise with the secular spirit of the time, that it had lost hold of its particular Christian values. Neither hot, like the nearby springs of Hierapolis (Pamukkale) nor cold, like refreshing spring water, the Christians at Laodicea were lukewarm, and the only value of such water was to make one vomit! But in spite of the harsh criticism, along with the judgement there is also the promise of a new way forward from the One who stands at the door and knocks.

Built during the 3rd century BC, Laodicea was named after Laodice, wife of Antiochus II, its founder. Having received little attention from archaeologists it is difficult for the Christian pilgrim of today to imagine anything of its ancient grandeur. Situated near the Lychus River, the city was located on major trading routes running east-west and north-south, and this helped to establish its reputation as a commercial centre. What remains to be seen today does not do justice to its past, but ruins of theatres, a gymnasium, a stadium, along with a nymphaeum and aqueduct, are dotted around the countryside.

Though not one of the seven churches, nearby **Hierapolis (Pamukkale)** is usually on the itinerary of most organised tours. Meaning 'Cotton Castle', Pamukkale is probably the best-known and most visited of all the hot springs in Turkey. The calcium-laden thermal waters have formed a remarkable white cascade stretching down the hillside, a great attraction drawing many visitors. Yet for the Christian pilgrim, Hierapolis itself is no less significant. Indeed, in Colossians 4:13, St. Paul refers to Epaphras working hard for the Christians in Colossae, Laodicea and Hierapolis.

Dating back to the 2nd century BC, Hierapolis is associated with the Apostle Philip, whose Martyrium has been discovered here. Also on site is an extensive cemetery, said to contain more than a thousand tombs, a Basilical Church, a ceremonial, triple-arched Gate, the Temple of Apollo and alongside this the Plutonium, a shrine honouring the god of the underworld. Further on up the hill is a well-preserved Roman theatre, and further on still is the Martyrium itself, though the tomb has not so far been discovered.

Istanbul

For most visitors to Western Turkey, some time spent in Istanbul will be regarded as a 'must'. Though, of course, not having any direct association with St. Paul himself, Istanbul, nonetheless, is an amazing city, with a fascinating blend of European and Asian cultures and styles. No visit here is likely to be a disappointment.

Strategically positioned on the Bosphorous and previously known as Byzantium, it was not until Constantine the Great built his new capital on the site and had it re-named Constantinople in AD 330, that full advantage of its splendid location was taken. Though the original intention had been to build the new capital at Troy on the Dardanelles, a change of mind sent the Emperor in the direction of Byzantium. However, in creating Constantinople his aim was not just to build a magnificent city rivalling the splendours of Rome, but also to establish it as a Christian capital city for the new Christian empire.

Constantinople soon developed into the great metropolis of the eastern empire and the Byzantine era continued to flourish, reaching its zenith during the time of Justinian (AD 527-565) as a city of great magnitude and opulence. The Byzantine Empire lasted for nearly a further thousand years but increasingly became a shadow of its early glories. The arrival of the Ottoman Empire in the 15th century heralded the final eclipse of Constantinople and the Empire that went with it. Under the Turks Istanbul was born.

But the city today is not just a monument to its rich and varied past, though there is plenty to mark that history. Istanbul is very much a vibrant, developing, modern city, which amply repays time spent there.

Obviously the Christian pilgrim will want to seek out some of the particular sites associated with Christianity. However, with the exception of one Byzantine church, at some stage all the others have been converted into mosques and this is the case with one of Istanbul's great showpieces, **St. Sophia** (or, Aya Sofia), a place which is sacred to both Christians and Moslems. The present building is the third to be erected on this site. The first church was built in AD 360 during the time of Constantinus, the son of Constantine, but it was destroyed by

ABOVE: *St. Sophia*
BELOW: *Mosaic in St Sophia*

fire in AD 404. Its successor in AD 415 was again destroyed by fire in AD 532. The present Justinian basilica was begun shortly after and when completed in AD 537 was regarded as a marvel for its time. Nothing like it had ever been previously attempted or even envisaged. It remained a Christian church until the Turkish occupation of Istanbul in the 15th century, when it was transformed into a mosque. Finally, in 1933, it became a museum.

The vastness of the nave, plus the size and height of the dome, are strikingly impressive as, too, are the mosaics, though some of them are very dimly-lit. For example, above the main doorway is a mosaic depicting Jesus, Mary and the Archangel Gabriel and in the apse above where the altar would have stood is one of Mary and the infant Jesus. Some of the most easily viewable mosaics are in the upper galleries, such as the one portraying Jesus, Mary and John the Baptist and dated during the 14th century. Indeed, the mosaics on view today date mostly from the 9th century onwards.

The one Byzantine church which has never been converted into a mosque is that of St. Irene ('Divine Peace'). Not far from St. Sophia it stands in the grounds of the Topkapi Palace. Believed to be Constantine's first cathedral until the building of St. Sophia, St. Irene was the venue for the meetings of the Second Ecumenical Council in AD 381. During the Ottoman period the building served as an arsenal and military museum, but these days is not generally open to the public, except for concerts during the Istanbul Festival.

Staying with the Byzantine theme, a visit to the Byzantine or Basilica Cisterns is highly recommended. Diagonally across from St. Sophia and built by Justinian in AD 532 to house the imperial water supply, the 336 columns in these underground cisterns give you the impression of being in a huge Basilica. With piped classical music and subdued lighting, a walk around the cisterns is one of the highlights of a visit to Istanbul.

In terms of religious buildings, the Blue Mosque should not be missed by any visitor. Situated opposite St. Sophia, it was built for Sultan Ahmet I between 1609 and 1617. With its domes, six minarets (the only mosque to have this number) and 260 windows, it is indeed impressive. But most striking of all is the interior, decorated with many thousands of blue Iznik tiles and it is from these that it takes its popular name.

However, perhaps even more elegant and splendid is the mosque of

Buying a carpet

Suleyman the Magnificent. Constructed between 1550 and 1557, it stands majestically on a hill, dominating the skyline on the Golden Horn's west bank. With four gracefully slender minarets at each corner of the courtyard, the mosque is a model of proportion and perfection. Everything about it from its columns, arches and stained glass windows gives the impression of being just right. There are those who recommend that if you have time to visit only one of the imperial mosques in Istanbul, this should be the one.

Equally demanding of the visitor's time is the Topkapi Palace. Such are the treasures on view, that for those who are particularly interested a whole day could be spent here. Once the home of the Ottoman rulers, the Palace is built round a series of courtyards. On entering through the main, stone gate, the visitor is inside the first courtyard, a park-like area, and it is here, on the left, that the church of St. Irene can be seen. At the end of this first courtyard is another gateway where you buy your tickets, and once through here you are in the main body of the Palace.

The second courtyard contains on one side, the Harem, which consists of a group of buildings and courtyards where the wives and concubines of the sultans lived separated from the rest of the Palace, and on the other side, the Palace Kitchens. On display is a wonderful collection of silver and priceless Chinese porcelain.

The third courtyard houses an exhibition of the various treasures of the sultans, with vessels and weapons adorned with the most fabulous jewels. Here is the famous Emerald Dagger as featured in the film 'Topkapi', but even this is no match for the stunning 86-carat Spoon Diamond. So magnificent is this display of gems that it is almost overpowering as you walk through the four rooms, taking in splendour after splendour. Also in this section of the Palace can be seen the various robes worn by the sultans and their families, and in another part of the courtyard is the Pavilion of the Holy Mantle, preserving various relics of the Prophet Mohammed. Beyond this fourth courtyard there is an outer one which houses the Archaeology Museum, which contains one of the most famous of all *sarcophogi*, the Alexander sarcophogus, depicting various scenes from his life and regarded as a particularly fine example of late Roman sculpture. In addition there are bronze pedestals, coats of arms, Greek and Roman bronzes, as well as impressive Trojan jewellery. Two other buildings accommodate the Museum of the Ancient Orient, with finds from Turkey and the Middle East, and the Tiled Kiosk, with a fine display of Turkish ceramics. This outer part of the Palace provides magnificent views over the Sea of Marmara and the Bosphorus. There is also a very good restaurant.

A book of this particular nature cannot begin to deal with Istanbul as comprehensively as it deserves and all we can do is point out some of its highlights. Depending on how long you stay here, highly recommended is a cruise on the Bosphorus, whose waters divide Asia from Europe, as well as visits to the Spice Market and the famous Kapali Carsi or Covered Bazaar. This latter is the largest Oriental market in the world, a labyrynth of streets and shops, where you can try your skill at haggling! Whether your interest is a piece of jewellery, decorated pottery, leather goods or leather clothing, or some simple souvenir of your visit to Istanbul, you are sure to find it here.

The Blue Mosque

Bargains from the Bazaar

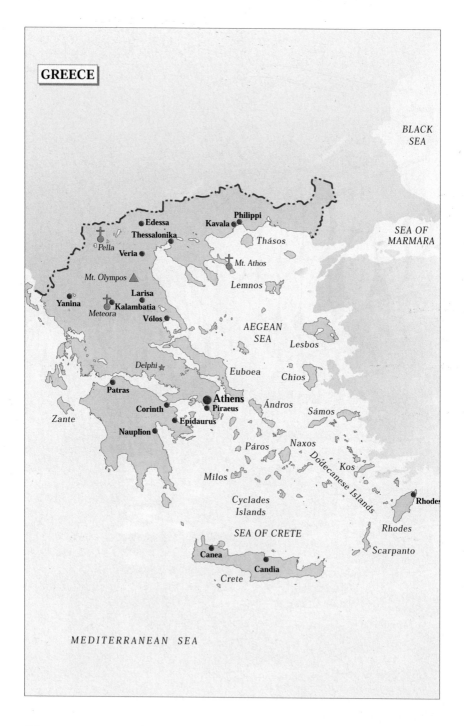

GREECE

BLACK
SEA

Edessa
Kavala
Philippi
Thessalonika
SEA OF
MARMARA
Pella
Veria
Thásos

Mt. Athos

Mt. Olympos

Lemnos

Larisa
Yanina
Kalambatia
Meteora
Vólos
AEGEAN
SEA
Lesbos

Delphi
Euboea
Chios

Patras
Athens
Ándros
Corinth
Piraeus
Sámos
Zante
Epidaurus
Nauplion
Páros
Naxos
Kos
Milos
Dodecanese Islands
Cyclades
Islands
Rhode

SEA OF CRETE
Rhodes

Canea
Scarpanto
Candia
Crete

MEDITERRANEAN SEA

42

PART 3

St Paul in Greece

For many contemporary visitors to Greece it is the islands rather than the mainland which is the prime attraction, for sun, sand and sailing. However, for the Christian pilgrim it is the mainland which is the principal inducement.

As noted in Part 1, it was while St. Paul was in Troas on his second missionary journey that he received the vision beckoning him to go over to Macedonia (Acts 16:8-10). By responding in the way he did, Paul expanded the range of the gospel from Asia Minor into Europe and eventually, of course, into the heart of the Empire, Rome.

Historical Background

Greece's history is long and varied, from the Minoan civilisation around 3000 BC, through Philip of Macedon and Alexander the Great, the Roman Empire, the Byzantine era, the Ottoman Empire, to the War of Independence in 1821 and ultimately to membership of the European Union in 1981. With such a richly accumulated past it seems invidious to select one particular period which marked the zenith of Greek civilization, but such a choice would undoubtedly be the Classical period. This was the great era of art, writing and philosophy, with names such as Aeschylus and Euripides, Herodotus and Thucydides, Socrates and Plato. During this period, too, the Parthenon was built, the Peloponnesian War between Athens and Sparta occurred, and the Oracle of Apollo at Delphi experienced its heyday in influencing political decisions. Along with much creativity there was also much upheaval. But the rise to power of Philip of Macedon in 359 BC brought the Classical period to an end. If quality was the hallmark of Classical Greece, it was quantity which most characteristically defined the Hellenistic period with the rapid expansion of the Greek-speaking world, particularly under Philip's son, Alexander the Great.

Though only aged 20 when he succeeded his father, Alexander possessed a driving ambition and a determined ruthlessness. So colossal were his triumphs that the Persians were defeated and a vast Empire

43

established. He was undoubtedly the major figure of this period of Greek history. Even though he died in 323 BC at the early age of 33, his achievements belied the brevity of his life. Despite the fact that there was no one of comparable stature to follow him, the Hellenistic era continued to thrive until the advent of the Romans at the beginning of the 2nd century BC.

Although Greece was regarded by the Romans as a centre of culture and learning, with Athens in particular as its focal point, it was, however, a time of general decline in prosperity. Nonetheless, on the plus side, the influence of Rome particularly during the reign of Augustus, brought a much-needed time of peace and stability. Then, with the coming of Constantine the Great and the founding of the new eastern capital of Constantinople, the Roman Empire divided into the Latin-speaking west and the Greek-speaking east. With the dawn of the Byzantine Empire, which took over from the old eastern Roman Empire and continued until 1453 when Constantinople was captured by the Ottomans, Greece became associated with Byzantine east. For most of this period the country was little more than a backwater and Athens a city with minimal influence.

Until the Greek War of Independence in 1821, the Greek state as such was in eclipse. Ruled by the Turks, the Orthodox Church was given an administrative responsibility for overseeing the Christian part of the population, for in the main the sultans regarded the Church as a useful vehicle for implementing Turkish law within the Christian community. This, in turn, gave the Church the opportunity to maintain the Greek identity through the survival of its culture and language.

But with the outbreak of the Greek War of Independence on 25th March 1821, Greece was eventually to establish itself again as an independent nation. Not that that solved everything. Many Greeks were dissatisfied with the slow progress towards prosperity, and political intrigue and in-fighting blighted its development. Indeed, it was not until 1832 that Greece was finally declared an independent kingdom. In one way or another conflict was to be the nation's continuing story whether World War I, or the disastrous attempt to conquer Constantinople in 1922, or occupation by the Germans, Italians and Bulgarians during World War II, or the Civil War of 1946-1949, or the military junta imposed by the Greek Colonels from 1967-1974. That is without mentioning the Cyprus problem during the 1950s and still a matter of issue between Greece and Turkey. Nowadays, of course, Greece is a democracy and a member of the European Union, but in 1981 even that decision was the cause of major division within the country.

But with spectacular scenery, wonderful weather, generous hospitality and, of course, magnificent Christian and Classical sites, the Greece of the 21st Century has much to inform and inspire the Christian pilgrim. Those seeking to follow the steps of St. Paul in this country of many contrasts and many delights will surely not be disappointed.

A good way of organising a tour to Greece is to fly into Thessalonika in the north and out from Athens in the south. This section of the book, therefore, begins in the north with Thessalonika and its associated sites, and then journeys south via the Meteora monasteries and Delphi. If time is short then it is possible to travel directly from Thessalonika to Athens, but should time not be at a premium, it is highly recommended to visit the amazing area of the monasteries and then Delphi, before finally arriving in Athens.

The White Tower at Thessalonika

Thessalonika

For the Christian pilgrim, Thessalonika provides a good centre for visiting not only the city itself, but also some of the other significant Pauline sites in the area, such as Philippi, Kavala (ancient Neapolis), the port where St. Paul landed after sailing from Troas, and Beroea (Veria), as well as the important Macedonian locations of Pella and Vergina. Beginning with Thessalonika itself, we then work our way outwards to the other places.

In antiquity **Thessalonika** was the capital of the Roman Province of Macedonia and is today the second city of the country. Founded in 315 BC by the Macedonian king, Kassander, and named after his wife, the city stood on the Via Egnatia, a major imperial route across northern Greece which linked Rome in the west with the Adriatic in the east. A thriving seaport, Thessalonika was a city of considerable importance and prosperity, and within it contained a notable Jewish community and synagogue. So it was a natural centre for St. Paul to visit on his second journey, accompanied by Silas.

His time in the region is described in Acts 16:11-17:14, beginning with the landing at Neapolis and ending with the departure from Beroea for Athens. This was in response to the vision in Troas where Paul believed he was being called to cross over from Asia Minor into Macedonia, the 'Macedonian Call', and in doing so to begin establishing Christianity in Europe.

The account of Paul's stay in Thessalonika as recorded in Acts is clearly a much-telescoped one, giving the impression that Paul may have been here only a very short time, whereas in reality it was probably a stay of several months. Indeed, from what he himself writes in his first letter to the Christians here, he appears to have stayed long enough to have established a church of some importance (I Thess. 1:6-10) and during that time performed manual work in order to sustain himself and not be a burden on the local folk (2 Thess. 3:8). Furthermore, he also received financial support from the Christians in Philippi (Phil. 4:16). Whatever the complete details of his stay in the city, it is apparent that he began with his usual strategy of preaching to the Jews. Though there was some success among them, it was the enthusiastic response of the Gentiles which provoked jealousy among the Jews and this in turn led to Paul and Silas moving on from Thessalonika to Beroea. Not too long after his visit to the city, Paul wrote his first letter to the church there, probably about AD 50 or 51 from Corinth, thus making it the earliest of his surviving letters and, furthermore, the earliest of any New Testament writing.

Though there is now no site in Thessalonika which is directly associated with Paul, there is more than enough to satisfy the particular interest of the Christian pilgrim. Churches abound, with the richest collection of Byzantine churches anywhere in Greece, including the largest anywhere in the country, Agios Dimitrios. Built originally in about AD 313, it was rebuilt after a fire in the 7th century, and again in the 20th century, though on a fifth-century plan, after the great fire of 1917. It celebrates the patron saint of Thessalonika, Dimitrios, who as a young man joined the Roman army but also converted to Christianity. However, when ordered to renounce his beliefs he refused and on the instruction of the Emperor Galerius, an infamous and ruthless persecutor of Christians, he was duly executed in AD 305. The crypt is believed to be the oldest surviving part of the church and marks the place where Dimitrios was put to death. In spite of past damage and the need for rebuilding, there are some remaining mosaics, probably from the early 7th century, and not surprisingly Dimitrios features in a number of them.

Nor should you miss the church of Agia Sofia, and people who have visited Istanbul will find it a reminder of the one-time church become mosque there. Only, in Thessalonika's case, what was built as a church in the mid-eighth century and became a mosque in the 16th, reverted to being a church in the 20th. Though somewhat stark in appearance from the outside, the interior is much more striking with mosaics and frescoes dating back to the 9th and 10th centuries. The most impressive of these is a large, well-preserved mosaic depicting the Ascension and set in the 98ft high dome.

Yet another church worth seeking out is that of Osios David, a comparatively small, fifth-century chapel which was once part of a large monastery. Behind the altar is a particularly fine mosaic representing the *Vision of Ezekiel* and which contains an unusual portrayal of a youthful Christ without a beard. There are other mosaics dating from the 12th century.

If there is the time and the inclination there are, of course, other churches deserving a visit, for example, the churches of Agioi Apostoli and Nikolaos Orfanos. Both have fine examples of religious art with some beautiful mosaics and frescoes. On the other hand, the Christian visitor following the steps of St. Paul through Greece is likely to have limited time and in addition will want to see other things in Thessalonika.

An absolute priority must be the Archaeological Museum which was opened in 1963. Here you can view Macedonian, Roman and Hellenistic finds from the area around, especially the stunning treasures discovered in the Royal tombs at Vergina. On display are sculptures, glittering jewellery, silver drinking cups and ivory miniatures, as well as crowns and armour belonging to King Philip II of Macedon, the father of Alexander the Great. Indeed, the museum contains the gold burial casket which held the bones of Philip. It is a truly remarkable collection of ancient discoveries and most definitely not to be omitted from any itinerary.

For those who are interested, situated just behind the Archaeological Museum is the Museum of Byzantine Culture, opened in 1995, with displays of Byzantine icons from the 15th to the 19th centuries, and there is also some splendid jewellery. Another fascinating visit can be made to the Folklore and Ethnological Museum, with exhibits from the last 250 years of Greece's national history. There are weapons, household utensils, national costumes, jewellery, plus accounts of rural and religious festivals, along with a photographic portrait of Thessalonika in the early 20th century.

One further location which most visitors will want to explore is the White Tower, probably Thessalonika's most famous landmark. No longer white in colour, it appears to have taken that description from an infamous event in 1826 when mutinous Janissaries, the Sultan's guard, were massacred. In consequence it became known as the 'Bloody Tower', though when the resulting evidence of the massacre was whitewashed out, it took its current name. The several floors and small circular rooms of the museum contain an exhibition of coins, pottery, mosaics, fragments of frescoes, column capitals, ritual burial offerings and ecclesiastical objects, all covering the period from about AD 300 to 1430. The spiral stairs around the rooms lead up to the roof, which affords a fine view over the city.

Macedonia

Eastern Macedonia

South-east of Thessalonika lies the region of **Halkidiki**, a peninsula consisting of three finger-like peninsulas jutting out into the Aegean Sea. A region of hills, valleys, trees and beaches, it is a popular holiday area. One of its most distinguished features, however, situated at the southern end of the most easterly peninsula, is Mount Athos, a collection of monasteries some of which date back to the 10th century. For more than 1000 years a community of monks has lived the daily life and religious practices of the Byzantines. At the moment there are about 20 monasteries functioning, and anyone fortunate enough to visit will be impressed by the frescoes and mosaics, the rich libraries and the precious art miniatures. That said, it is not easy to gain access to the monasteries and, indeed, women are strictly forbidden. A view from a boat trip around the peninsula is the nearest most people will get.

In general, itineraries may not have time to include even the sail around Mount Athos and will concentrate on driving eastwards across the northern part of the region along by the sea and beaches to **Kavala**, founded in the 6th century BC and identified with the port of Neapolis as the first place in Europe on which which St. Paul set foot. Today it is a bustling city built around its harbour, though originally it was the port which served nearby Philippi. For the Christian pilgrim on a day excursion to Philippi from Thessalonika, Kavala may be little more than a coffee or lunch-stop, but a very pleasant place in which to experience either. There are certainly no reminders of Paul's landing here, but if there is time to wander around, the 16th century Turkish aqueduct should not be missed.

A short drive inland is **Philippi**, named by Philip II. One of its claims to fame is that of being the scene, in 42 BC, of a great battle between the forces of Brutus and Cassius, both of whom had taken part in the assassination of Julius Caesar two years previously, and those of Antony and Octavian, whose armies were victorious in the engagement. By the time St. Paul visited Philippi (Acts 16:11-40) it

Philippi

had become thoroughly Romanised, and as the first main stop on the Egnatian Way from Asia to the Adriatic, had developed into an important city.

The conversion of Lydia, from Thyatira in Asia Minor and famous for its luxurious purple cloth, enabled the missionaries to establish a base in Philippi due to the hospitality she provided for them. Paul's own letter to the church here, written some time later, indicates that he founded a thriving Christian community. As already noted, the church was most generous in the financial support it contributed to the apostle during his stay in Thessalonika. Indeed, the letter he wrote to the Philippians conveys the warmth he felt for them.

The visit of Paul and Silas to the city is also notable for the exorcism of a slave girl, which led to the apostles being beaten and imprisoned, then eventually escaping during an earthquake, an event seen as miraculous, leading as it did to the conversion and baptism of the jailer and his family. This becomes the spur for the apostles to move on, but not without an apology from the local magistrates who have broken the law by beating Roman citizens.

The ruins at Philippi are extensive. On one side of the road lie the remains of a 5th century church, with aisles, transepts and a semicircular apse. Near here also is said to be the prison where Paul and Silas were kept. Before leaving the ruins on this side of the road there is the Theatre, originally of Greek design but later re-styled to suit the Romans. The majority of what can be seen today is a reconstruction, with just a few original Roman tiers.

Crossing the road brings you to the main and, indeed, more interesting part of the site. Here is the Forum, dating back to the time of Marcus Aurelius. Though the remains do not reach any great height, the fertile imagination can soon build up a picture, using the foundations of two temples and a library. Note, too, the great size of many of the stones and slabs. Presumably it was here that St.Paul did some of his preaching. But the most impressive remains are those of another Basilica, built during the reign of Justinian (AD 527-565). This was intended to be an architectural masterpiece, a great domed church, but during the construction, the dome above the sanctuary collapsed and the building was never completed. But there is more than enough still available to interest the visitor, with piers, columns and sculptured decorations. Also to be seen on the site are a large number of marble seats which constituted the public toilet! Before leaving the area it is worth driving a short distance from the site where a shrine beside a stream commemorates the baptism of Lydia.

On the way back to Thessalonika a short detour to view the Lion of Amphipolis is recommended. This is an enormous statue of a lion, with a splendid mane and glaring eyes, which was re-assembled from 4th century fragments and guards the mouth of the river Strymon. It really is a magnificent representation of a lion and more than probably observed by St. Paul as he passed through Amphipolis on his way from Philippi to Thessalonika.

Western Macedonia

If necessary the main sites in this area can be covered in one long day tour, Pella, Edessa, Veria, and Vergina. The only site associated with St. Paul is **Veria** (New Testament Beroea in Acts 17:10-14). Lying south of the Via Egnetia it possessed a flourishing Jewish community, among whom Paul found a more ready and receptive audience than in Thessalonika. Gentiles, too, along with Jews, responded eagerly to the Christian message and many became believers. It was only when Jews from Thessalonika, hearing of what was happening in Beroea, came there to incite trouble, that the apostle was encouraged by the new believers to move on.

Here, too, there is nothing directly associated with Paul's visit. There are remains of Roman fortifications and various post-Byzantine churches, the most important of which is the 14th century Church of Christou, with some elegant and colourful frescoes. For all its association with St. Paul, Veria is a place which the Christian pilgrim will probably do little more than pause in, to mark the location as it were, on the way to Vergina.

For those who are interested in Macedonian history and discovery, **Vergina**, however, will be a different story. It was here, just outside this small village, that during the 20th century some of the most momentous Greek finds were made, in particular, the Royal Tombs of King Philip of Macedonia and other members of the royal family. Excavations began in 1976 and yielded unimaginable treasures. Among these were two gold caskets containing his and maybe even the queen's bones, beautiful gold jewellery, armour and statuettes, all of which can be viewed in Thessalonika's Archaeological Museum. Nearby are more tombs known as the Macedonian Tombs. A short distance from here, set on a mound, are the foundations of the Palace of Palatitsia. Though again there is nothing of any great height, there is enough to give an idea of the layout and enormous dimensions of the palace. Still to be seen in situ is a beautiful mosaic floor. Although the palace is dated in the 3rd century BC, it is believed that the site may have been occupied as far back as 1000 BC. One can only begin to guess at the wealth of treasures yet to be unearthed.

Finally, the two other places previously mentioned as part of a tour in Western Macedonia. The first is **Pella**, northwest from Thessalonika, and once the capital of Macedonia. A royal city, it was the residence of King Philip and the birthplace of his son, Alexander the Great, in 356 BC, who was also tutored here by the philosopher, Aristotle.

The smallness of the site belies its ancient glories and should not, therefore, be underestimated. It is particularly famous for its pebble mosaics, some of the finest in Greece, both in the site itself and in the museum. Depicting mostly hunting scenes and dating back to about 300 BC, they are full of life and colour. Particularly outstanding are

The shrine to Lydia

Dionysus riding on a panther, the Lion Hunt, and the Stag Hunt. The first two are both located in the House of the Lion Hunt (taking its name from the mosaic), built around the end of the 4th century BC, its size suggesting that it was probably some important official residence. Also to be seen are the Agora and the area where the shops were located. This, too, is another site where there is much excavation yet to be done and remember, don't forget to look in the Museum!

It is worth driving on from here to **Edessa,** if only to see its waterfalls. The oldest remain to be seen is an arched bridge over which the Via Egnetia passed. But most people come here for the waterfalls, which cascade down from the town to the valley below. In any case, after an early visit to Pella it makes a very pleasant coffee stop on the way to Veria and Vergina.

South to Athens

If, like St. Paul, the Christian pilgrim has begun in the north of the country, then after exploring Thessalonika and Macedonia, it will be time to head south for Athens. One way to do this is by rail directly between the two cities, which is quick and convenient if there is pressure of time. However, if there is no such pressure, then the alternative route by road is thoroughly recommended. Part of the attraction of this route is that it passes by Mount Olympos, a range of peaks spanning some 12 miles and the legendary home of Zeus and the other Greek gods. Another advantage is that you can stay overnight in Kalambaka and next morning visit the spectacular **Meteora Monasteries**.

The first view of the rocks on which the monasteries are situated is really so stunning as to be not easily forgotten. This amazing, sculptured formation of rocks rises up from the plain of Thessalia, with the monasteries perched among them like eagles-nests. Indeed, the very name 'Meteora' refers to the way in which they seem to be suspended in the air. Originally twenty-four in number, they date back to the early 14th century, but from at least the 10th century the rocks had been home to hermits. One can only marvel at the way in which they were built, with everything hauled up by basket and rope ladder, stones, brick, wood, from the valley below. Today, however, there are only six which are accessible to the general public, most of the others having fallen into disuse and ruin by the end of the 18th century. Please note that it is essential for visitors to dress appropriately with no shorts for either women or men, and no bare shoulders.

If you were to spend a whole day here it would be possible to inspect all six monasteries, but in reality you will have half-a-day at the most. So, which ones should be chosen? Well, without doubt, the number one priority must be the Mega Meteoron, the oldest and the highest, and also known as the Monastery of the Transfiguration. Its domed church is truly glorious, with strikingly colourful frecoes depicting the history, dogma and liturgy of the Greek Orthodox Church. There is also a representation of Athanasius, the founder of the monastery, holding a model of the church. Other treasures on display in the monastery are ancient manuscripts on parchment, silver liturgical vessels and very fine icons, dating from the 14th to the 16th centuries. As can be imagined, the views from Mega Meteoron across the area around are really quite something. By the way, if you wonder about all the steps up to the Monastery, well, just think that up until 1923 you would have had to go by rope ladders and then be hoisted up in a net!

Nearby is the **Monastery of Varlaam**, founded in 1518 by two brothers, but said to be named after the first hermit who lived on this rock in 1350. Situated in attractive gardens the monastery's church is dedicated to All Saints and decorated with 16th century frescoes, which have subsequently been restored. Among the frescoes is one of its founders, Theophanis and Nectarios. Once again there are many treasures on view - crosses, vestments, silver liturgical vessels, manuscripts on parchment and hundreds of books. Also displayed in the museum is a Book of Gospels, dating back to the first half of the 10th century. On the outside of the building notice the ascent tower by

The Monasteries at Meteora

which goods and people used to be hauled up on a rope.

If visits to these two monasteries are not to be rushed, so that their respective treasures may be savoured, there may not be time to visit any of the other four - Holy Trinity, St. Nicholas Anapaphas, St. Stephen and Rousanou. But in exploring the first two at a leisurely pace, the Christian pilgrim will begin to appreciate why it is that the Meteora monasteries are so special. Interestingly enough, whilst not that many years ago there were only a handful of monks and nuns and, so it seemed, mainly for the benefit of the tourists, more recently increasing numbers have come to live, pray and work here, so continuing and enhancing the religious tradition of the monasteries.

It could be possible to do a long drive from here direct to Athens. On the other hand it may be considered a wiser option once more to break the journey by staying overnight in or near **Delphi**, so as to visit the site first thing the next morning before the tourist coaches from Athens, or even from the cruise ships in Itea, disgorge their hordes! An early morning visit is highly recommended, followed by the final part of the journey south into Athens.

Standing among hills and olive groves, the setting of Delphi is totally enchanting, to such an extent that some would describe it as the most attractive Classical site anywhere in Greece. It is a claim difficult to refute. Regarded by the ancient Greeks as the centre of the world, Delphi was believed to be the home of Apollo and individuals came from all over to seek guidance from the god about what courses of action they should take in particular circumstances.

To explore its beauty, start at the main entrance, which was once a market place, and follow the Sacred Way leading eventually to the remains of the Temple of Apollo. Originally this route was lined with something like 3000 statues and treasuries, so today's visitor must imagine how awe-inspiring the approach must have been. The treasuries were donated by various Greek city-states in appreciation for good fortune consequent upon favourable guidance from the Oracle. On the way up, to the left, are the foundations of the Sikyonian and Siphnian Treasuries. The route then takes a hairpin turn to the right, and there on the left is the Athenian Treasury, the first Doric construction to consist entirely of marble. Though not a large building, it is one of the landmarks of Delphi and was reconstructed in 1906. Adjacent to this is the Bouleuterion, the Council House, where policy was decided, and just beyond it the Rock of the Sybil, where according to legend, the first oracles were chanted by the priestess.

Eventually you arrive at the what remains of the Temple of Apollo, built originally in the 6th century BC, but what is seen today emanates from the 4th century BC. From the Temple is a wonderful panoramic view both of the site itself and the region around. Reconstruction, particularly in the form of three huge Doric columns, gives some impression of the scale and grandeur of the building.

Further up the hill beyond the Temple is the magnificent Theatre, originally constructed in the 4th century but later remodelled by the Romans. Blending into the hillside it provides a most wonderful setting for a theatre and held 5,000 people. If you still have energy left, a climb up to the top tiers for further breath-taking views is encouraged.

But don't consume all your energy as you will need some for the walk up to the highest point of Delphi, the Stadium, the best-preserved in the country. Every four years this was the scene of the Pythian Games, second only to those of Olympia. Poetry and music were also part of the occasion, for indeed, the games themselves grew out of a music festival. Some 658ft long, what is visible today comes from Roman times, with four remaining pillars from the Roman triumphal arch. As you look around you will notice that much of the seating is surprisingly well-conserved.

All the above relates to the upper part of the site, but if you retrace your steps to the main road and cross over, you will come to the lower part. Here is the Gymnasium, where athletes trained for the Pythian Games, and complete with the remains of changing rooms. But beyond this is probably the most beautiful of all Delphi's monuments, the circular *tholos*, once surrounded by 20 Doric columns but now with three re-constructed ones standing to illustrate its previous elegance. As well as the Sanctuary to Apollo, Delphi also had one to Athena. Set between the remains of two temples dedicated to the goddess, the *tholos* dates back to the early 4th century BC.

Before leaving, however, a visit to the Museum is advised, for its contents are second in importance only to those of the Acropolis in Athens. There are sculptures, pottery, bronzes, friezes, all portraying the history and beauty of Delphi. But the highlight of the exhibition is undoubtedly the life-size Bronze Charioteer from the 5th century BC.

The Athenian Treasury at Delphi

Athens

If this were a more general guidebook, Athens could warrant a whole publication to itself, there is so much to see and do. However, within the limitations we have set ourselves in this particular book, that it should be a portable and concise travelling companion for the Christian pilgrim, then all we can aim to do is highlight those aspects of the city which are most likely to appeal to someone following the steps of St. Paul through Greece and with limited time in Athens.

Though it has a history of more than 3,000 years, the golden age of the city was during the great Classical period of ancient Greece. Having emerged as a growing power during the 6th century BC, it was the 5th century which witnessed the great flowering of art and literature, and, of course, architecture, as under Perikles (495-429 BC) an ambitious programme of building was initiated. Yet during the era of Macedonian expansion, Athens began to be somewhat overshadowed, and by the time of St. Paul's arrival in the Roman age, it had lost most of its previous political power. It was, nevertheless, still regarded as the cultural and intellectual centre of the ancient world. But by the time of the Byzantine period, Athens was stripped of all its glory. So it remained until there was a revival of its fortunes in the 15th century after the Turkish invasion, and finally it began to re-establish itself on becoming the capital of Greece in 1834 after the War of Independence.

Although under the Romans Athens was no longer a political power to be reckoned with, it still had its architecture and art as reminders of its glorious past. Temples, altars and statues still abounded, and it was this multiplicity of objects of devotion to which Paul referred when he addressed the Athenians from the Areopagus, alluding to an inscription he had seen on one of their altars, 'To an unknown god' (Acts 17:16-34), though no altar has ever been found bearing that particular dedication. The reference may mean no more than altars erected to nameless gods, and there is evidence that this was a practice in Athens at that time. Apparently Paul's preaching met with no resounding success, but it was not a total failure as he left behind some individual converts.

The **Areopagus** is the name of a small hill, 'Mars Hill', near the Acropolis, and in the Classical period is believed to have been the place where the Supreme Court met. In Roman times it was still the name of an assembly, but whose precise function is not clear. Possibly it exercised control over religion and morals, or had some jurisdiction over the various philosophers and teachers. Whatever the case, the only reminder of Paul's address is a bronze plaque on which the text from 'Acts' is inscribed.

From here is access to the **Acropolis**, a natural fortification with strengthened walls on which was built the 'upper city'. Now, as then, the Acropolis dominates the life of the city and wherever you are in Athens it seems that you can never escape the looming presence of this great rock - your eyes always seem to be drawn towards it.

You enter the Acropolis proper through the remains of the Propylaia, the official grand entrance to the citadel. Regarded as a masterpiece of Classical architecture, it was commissioned by Perikles and begun in 437 BC. To the right of the Propylaia is the Temple of Athena Nike, built between 427-424 BC, to celebrate victory over the Persians and dedicated to Athena Nike, the goddess of Victory. Destroyed by the Turks in the 17th century it was restored two centuries later, with further major reconstruction in 1935.

Before moving on further, one other building should be observed from this entrance area. This part of the Acropolis affords the best vantage point from which to look down on the fine Roman Theatre of Herodes Atticus, built in AD 161 by the Roman consul, Herodes Atticus. Seating 5000 people it was originally enclosed under a cedar-wood roof. It was restored in 1955 and today hosts drama and music as part of the Athens Festival.

For most people the **Parthenon** symbolises not only the Acropolis but Athens itself. Built in 447 BC during the glorious period of Classical construction under Perikles, its ruins still stand today, though due to the ravages of weather and tourists, it is no longer accessible to the public. Erected as a temple, it was dedicated to the goddess Athena the Virgin ('Athena Parthenos') and contained a huge statue of her made from ivory and gold, of which a replica can be found in the National Archaeological Museum. During the 5th century AD it became a Christian basilica and in Turkish times was used as a mosque, complete with minaret. Not far from the Parthenon is a Museum containing finds from the Acropolis, including 5th

The Parthenon sits atop the Acropolis

century statues and remnants of the Parthenon frieze, though the most famous sculptures of all, the Elgin Marbles, are somewhat controversially housed in the British Museum, many people believing that Athens is their natural home.

If the Parthenon is a 'must' so, too, is the Erechtheion, situated on the most sacred part of the Acropolis and believed to be where Athena produced the first olive tree out of a rock in her struggle with Poseidon for sovereignty of the city. Named after Erechtheus, one of the mythical kings of Athens, it is built on different levels and adorned with Ionic columns and beautifully decorated capitals. Somewhat smaller than the neighbouring Parthenon, the Erechtheion is no less majestic, having been extensively restored after it was all but destroyed in 1827 during the War of Independence.

But before leaving the Acropolis, make sure you take in the views of the city around. To exit from here, though, you have to take the same way back through the Propylaia.

While in this vicinity you might like to take a look at the Theatre of

The Theatre of Herodes Atticus at the foot of the Parthenon

Dionysos, on the southern side of the Acropolis and cut into the rock. The plays of Aeschylus, Sophocles, Euripides and Aristophanes were first performed here, so heralding the beginnings of Greek tragedy.

Once you return to the city proper, make time to visit Hadrian's Arch. It marks the boundary between the old Greek city of Theseus and the new Roman city of Hadrian. Adjacent to it is the Temple of Olympian Zeus, the largest in Greece and larger even than the Parthenon. It was begun in the 6th century BC and completed by Hadrian in 132 AD. Only 15 of the original Corinthian columns remain, but their colossal height (58ft) gives some impression of the grandeur of the temple, which looks particularly striking when it is floodlit at night.

Museums are not to everyone's taste, but the **National Archaeological Museum** is probably one of the finest anywhere in the world. It has an excellent display of ancient statues, sculptures, Hellenistic bronzes, and busts of Emperors. There is also a huge presentation of pottery, some of the finest pieces dating back to the 5th century BC. But the highlight of the Museum must surely be the

Mycenaean collection, with quite stunning gold treasures dating from the 16th century BC, as well as the famous gold Mask of Agamemnon. The gold objects on display here are breathtaking and a tribute to ancient jewellers, potters and goldsmiths. The treasures which can be viewed are just too numerous to detail, but in total present a wonderful exhibition of the history of Greek art.

Other museums which may interest you are the **Museum of Cycladic Art**, a delightful display of the remarkable works of art produced in the Cyclades from about 3000 BC, with some exceptional small statues; the **Byzantine Museum**, covering 1500 years of Byzantine art with a splendid array of icons, ecclesiastical relics, and frescoes rescued from various churches; and the Benaki Museum, with a diverse collection of ceramics, carvings, costumes and jewellery, ranging from the 3rd century BC through to the 20th century, as well as some El Greco paintings.

Every visitor to Athens will want to discover the Plaka, one of the older parts of modern Athens. Busy, lively, bustling, it is not necessarily the tourist trap it is sometimes made out to be. Most people visit here more than once. The Plaka is rather like a large market and is a good place to come and browse round the shops, some dealing in antiques, others in tourist souvenirs. You can also find many small studios where icons are painted using traditional methods. In addition to all this, when you are feeling hungry there are plenty of tavernas where you can eat.

While in this region look for the tiny, domed, 12th century church of Panagia Gorgoepikoos, next to the Cathedral and dwarfed by it. This really is a little gem and is sometimes known as 'The Little Cathedral'. In size it is no more than 24.5ft by 39.5ft, which would probably have been appropriate in the 12th century when Athens was little more than a village. The outside is decorated with friezes and bas-reliefs spanning Classical to Byzantine periods.

Also in the Plaka is one of its favourite parish churches, Agios Nikolaos Ragavas, on the corner of Prytaneiou and Epicharmou. Originally a Byzantine church dating back to the 11th century, rebuilt in the 18th and restored in 1970, it is a very popular place for Greek weddings.

If you have spare time in Athens and fancy a short cruise, Piraeus is, of course, its main port and one of the busiest in the Mediterranean. It is possible to take a day cruise from here to some of the nearby islands.

Corinth and the Peloponnese

From Athens it is possible to make a day excursion to Corinth and either, or both, Epidaurus and Mycenae, via the **Corinth Canal**. Completed in 1893 after 12 years of building, it was the Emperor Nero who first had the idea of building a canal to save ships sailing all the way round the Peloponnese. However, though the project was begun by him it was never finished. Unfortunately, these days it is no longer wide enough to take the supertankers and giant container ships but smaller vessels can still be seen sailing through. It is possible to park nearby and look down some 90 metres on to the canal from the walkway across the road bridge.

The major Christian site is, of course, **Corinth**, destroyed by the Romans in 146 BC, and then rebuilt as a colony a century later by Julius Caesar. It developed as a prosperous city due to its location between the Corinthian and Saronic gulfs, for bringing goods across the isthmus was the shortest and safest route between east and west. To save ships making the risky voyage around the Peloponnese, cargoes were unloaded on one side of the isthmus then carried over to the other and reloaded. At its height the city reached a population of 750,000 and excavations have demonstrated its extent, but it was eventually destroyed by earthquakes during the Byzantine era.

St. Paul's founding of the church in Corinth is described in Acts 18. He spent eighteen months here round about AD 50-51, practising his trade as a tent-maker to support his preaching mission, though once again he was not without his opponents, both Jews and Gentiles. The population at that time was extremely cosmopolitan, consisting of Romans, Greeks and Jews, but the city had gained a reputation for its immorality. The apostle's first letter to the church here describes a flourishing Christian community, in spite of the various problems referred to in his correspondences with them, for clearly the 'first' letter available to us is not in fact the first that he wrote to them (see 1 Cor. 5:9). In addition to the various theological and moral issues raised in the letters, Paul also had to deal with challenges to his own authority as an apostle.

There are two parts of the site, ancient Corinth and Acrocorinth, the latter set on a hill some distance away from the main site. One of the most prominent buildings at the lower level is the Temple of Apollo, one of the oldest in Greece, dating from the 6th century BC, and preserved by the Romans when they rebuilt the city in AD 44. There are still seven massive Doric columns standing. Another such structure is the Temple of Octavia, dedicated to the sister of the Emperor Augustus, but all that remains are three Corinthian columns.

It is also possible to make out the sprawling remains of the Agora, in which you can identify the location of some of the shops, as well as the Bema, or Roman Governor's tribune, before which Paul was brought when he was charged with sacrilege by the Jews. To reach the Agora you walk along Lechaion Way, which linked Corinth with the port of Lechaion. The road entered the city through a gateway and would have been bordered by shops. Just by the gateway is an attractive monument, the Fountain of Peirene.

Near the entrance and just south of the Odeon, is the Museum, in which are displayed various discoveries from the site. There are statue heads, vases and 2nd century Roman mosaics from nearby villas.

All the time you are looking around Corinth, you cannot but be aware of the towering presence of **Acrocorinth.** Whether you will have time to visit it depends on other elements of your itinerary if you are just on a day excursion from Athens. Entrance to the upper city is through three gateways, one Turkish, one Frankish and the third Byzantine. The whole place is surrounded by a formidable set of fortifications and within them are the remains of houses, churches and mosques. As you can imagine, the views all around from such a vantage point are stupendous.

From Corinth it is a short journey to **Mycenae,** and you may already have enjoyed its wonderful treasures on display in Athens. Represented here is a remarkable civilization spanning some 600 years from 1700-1100 BC. You will need to use your imagination to make the most of this forbidding citadel, for most of what remains is in the form of foundations. There is, however, the imposing Lion Gate, so-called because of the sculptured lions above the lintel, and through which you pass into the stronghold. Here are remains of the Palace, royal graves, houses and a flight of steps leading down to a cistern which was connected to a spring outside the citadel, so assuring those inside of a water supply during times of siege. Even if you don't visit the site, make sure you visit the Archaeological Museum!

Whether or not Mycenae is on your itinerary, **Epidaurus** most certainly should be. A religious and therapeutic centre dedicated to the

The Lechaion Way, looking towards Acrocorinth

Corinthian columns of the Temple of Octavia at Corinth

god Asklepion, it is, however, probably most renowned for what could be described as the most beautiful of all Greek theatres. With 55 tiers of seats it is capable of holding 14,000 people. The lower 34 tiers are original and date back to the 4th century BC, while the upper 21 tiers belong to the Roman age. A unique feature is that of all theatres it is the only one extant from antiquity with a circular orchestra. While you are there you may well hear someone demonstrating its incomparable acoustic, provided there is not too much hubbub from the other tourists! During a quiet spell, and there are not too many of those, you will be able to hear from the very top tier.

If it is possible to squeeze in a visit to **Nauplion** then do, even if just for a brief stop. It is a thoroughly delightful and elegant little port looking across a huge bay. Above the town and standing like a sentinel over it, is a Venetian castle.

Hopefully, once you have explored this part of the peninsula, your drive back to Athens will be via the coastal route. It is extremely beautiful, with wonderful glimpses of the coastline, and leads you back across the Corinth Canal.

St Paul in Malta

Not more than 17 miles by 9 miles at its widest points, the island of Malta has a rich tapestry of history out of all proportion to its size. At a maritime crossroads in the Mediterranean, the occupying Phoenicians, Carthaginians, Romans, Arabs and British have all played their part in shaping its chequered history. Nor, of course, must the considerable influence of the Knights of St. John be overlooked, who for nearly 270 years, from 1530-1798, dominated the life and character of the island. For today's visitor there is still much on the island to illustrate the influence of the Knights, particularly in Vittoriosa, their first base when they arrived in Malta.

That being said, much of the current character of the island dates back to an unexpected and accidental visit in AD 60, an event of no less significance for Malta than all its other momentous happenings. The preaching of St. Paul in the Holy Land, especially in Jerusalem and Caesarea, had caused so much opposition from the local religious leaders, that he was arrested by the Romans, probably for his own safety as much as anything else. But at his trial Paul, as a Roman citizen, exercised his right of appeal to the Emperor, with the result that he and St. Luke were shipped as prisoners from Caesarea to Rome.

However, during the journey the ship was hit by a violent storm just off the north-east coast of Malta and ran aground. Nevertheless, all 276 people on board landed safely. 'After we had reached safety, we then learned that the island was called Malta. The natives showed us unusual kindness. Since it had begun to rain and was cold, they kindled a fire and welcomed all of us around it' (Acts 28:1-2). The rest of the chapter sketches an outline of Paul's three-month stay on the island and subsequent onward journey to Rome. Indeed, the whole story of the events leading up to Paul's arrest in Caesarea and eventual arrival in Rome may be read in Acts 21-28.

For the Christian pilgrim of today the spot identified as the site of the landing is said to be St. Paul's Islands, just off St. Paul's Bay. There are two islands, the larger one of which has a very prominent statue of St. Paul, commemorating the reputed spot where he stepped ashore. It is possible, when the sea is not too rough, to take a cruise round the islands from St. Paul's Bay. Here, on the mainland of the Bay between Bugibba and Xemxija, is St. Paul's Church, an elegant building with traces of neo-Baroque and Gothic, whose striking interior contains an inevitable painting of the shipwreck. It is said to be built on the site where the Apostle was bitten by a viper, threw it into the fire and miraculously suffered no harm. A short distance away in the direction of Xemxija is Ghan Razul, or 'the Apostle's Fountain', where, according to tradition, St. Paul either baptised the first Maltese Christian, or where he struck a rock and drank the water which came from it.

M'dina/Rabat

Not far inland is the 'silent city' of **M'dina**, so-called because for many years its narrow streets were regarded as unsuitable for traffic and even today only residents may drive in with cars. Once the capital of Malta, under the Knights it relinquished that status to Valletta.

M'dina is traditionally associated with Publius, the Roman Governor of the island at the time of Paul's visit, who welcomed the Apostle to his home and offered him hospitality for three days. During this time the father of Publius was sick with a fever, but was healed by Paul. According to tradition, not only was Publius converted to Christianity but was also made the first bishop of Malta

Legend has it that the present day Cathedral, St. Paul's Cathedral, is built on the site of the house on which the father of Publius lived, replacing the first church built on the site in the 12th or 13th century and destroyed by an earthquake in 1693. Built between 1697 and 1702 by Lorenzo Gafà, the new Cathedral is regarded as his most outstanding piece of work and a superb example of Baroque art. Though the exterior has an impressive facade, fronted by a pair of cannon dating back to the time of the Knights, it is the interior which shows the building at its most splendid.

Designed in the shape of a Latin cross, with a central vaulted nave and two aisles, the interior is richly decorated with paintings on the ceiling, the altar and in the apse, depicting various scenes from the life of St. Paul, including the shipwreck. The colourful marble mosaic floor covers the tombs of some of the leading Maltese ecclesiastics and nobles. The marble font and the carved wooden sacristy both date back to the earlier Cathedral and are the only remains from it. Surmounted by a magnificent Baroque dome, visible from and

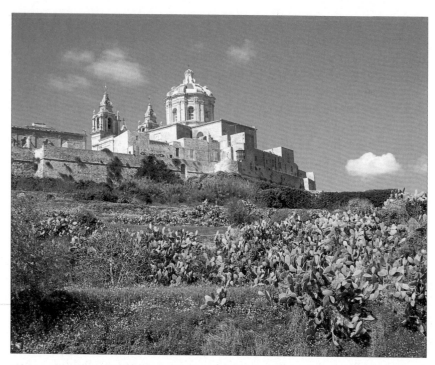

The ancient capital of M'dina

dominating the countryside for miles around, the whole building is an architectural and artistic masterpiece.

Also worth a visit is the adjacent Cathedral Museum, which contains much from the previous Cathedral, including Papal Bulls and beautifully illuminated choirbooks dating back to the 11th century. In addition there is a splendid collection of coins, from Carthage to the modern, as well as woodcuts by Dürer and engravings by Goya.

If there is time, take the opportunity to wander round the narrow streets and soak up the atmosphere of this delightful place, with its palaces, monasteries and churches.But make sure to find Bastion Square, because from here is a wonderful panorama of the island, encompassing both St. Paul's Bay and Valletta. Notice, too, the dome of **Mosta Church**, dedicated to St. Mary and said to be the fourth largest unsupported dome in the world. Built in the 19th century its other main claim to fame is that on the 9th April 1942, a German bomb crashed through the dome during a service with more than 300 people in the congregation. Miraculously the bomb did not explode, and a replica of the bomb as well as photos of the damage caused, can be seen in the sacristy. Well worth a visit.

Though larger in size and population than M'dina, the adjoining neighbourhood of **Rabat** is, in fact, a suburb. Tradition suggests that this was where Paul spent the three months of his stay in Malta and the deeply-rooted Christian beliefs of the Maltese people today clearly bear witness to the success of the Apostle's time on the island. In the heart of Rabat is St. Paul's Church, reputedly built on the site of Publius's house and also said to be the first recognised parish church on the island. Below the church is St. Paul's Grotto, where he is believed to have spent the winter of his stay. Here there is a marble statue of the Apostle and various frescoes. A short distance away are the Catacombs of St. Paul and of St. Agatha, the latter having fled from Sicily to avoid her tormentors and taking up residence in Rabat. Both are full of tombs, niches and canopies cut from stone, which suggests that in the 4th and 5th centuries quite a large Christian community lived here though, of course, there is no direct association with Paul himself.

Valletta

With the arrival of the Knights in 1530, Valletta rather than M'dina was eventually to become the capital of Malta, but not until building began in 1566 under the orders of Grand Master St. Jean de la Valette. Founded in the 11th century, the Order of the Knights of St. John of Jerusalem was established principally to provide medical care for pilgrims to the Holy Land. But in time the role of the Order developed into a military task of fighting the infidel, with pilgrims needing physical protection as well as medical care. Eventually in 1291, along with the remaining Crusaders, the Knights were thrown out of the Holy Land, finally conquering and settling on the island of Rhodes in 1310. Here they stayed until 1522, when they were finally defeated by the Turks.

After agreeing an honourable surrender with the Turkish Sultan, Suleyman (known in the future as Suleyman the Magnificent), the Knights left Rhodes and were without any permanent home until Charles V, Emperor of Spain, offered them a refuge in Malta. So it was that in October 1530, under Grand Master L'Isle Adam, the Knights arrived at their new home and settled in Birgu (now Vittoriosa).

This area, known as the Three Cities, (Senglea, Cospicua and Vittoriosa) was regarded by the Knights as their capital and, therefore, the island's capital. So it remained until the Great Siege of 1565 when, under the leadership of La Valette, a totally outnumbered defence of Knights, Maltese Militia, Spanish and Italian foot soldiers, faced an overwhelming number of Turkish invaders, sent by Suleyman the Magnificent against an island stronghold which stood between the Turks and their domination of the entire Mediterranean Sea. Beginning in the May of that year, the siege was finally lifted in September after one of the most courageous defensive stands in military history. The Turks left, never to return, and so, in the light of the siege, La Valette determined to build an impressive new capital which would also be a fortified stronghold. In May 1566 work began on building Valletta.

There are a number of remarkable churches in the city, but for the Christian visitor one most certainly to be discovered is that of St. Paul's Shipwreck, in St. Paul Street. Dating back originally to the 17th century, the church is lavishly designed, especially the gold and silver of the ornate Chapel of the Blessed Sacrament. This was the work of Lorenzo Gafà, the architect of M'dina Cathedral, and his brother, Melchiorre, was responsible for the wooden gilded statue of St. Paul, which is carried through the streets on the 10th February each year to commemorate the date of the shipwreck. The ceiling frescoes portray incidents from his time on the island. The church also contains part of a reputed wristbone of the Apostle, as well as a piece of the block from Rome on which he is said to have been beheaded. Be that as it may, a visit to the church is not to be missed.

Another absolute must is St. John's Co-Cathedral, so-called because of the status and distinction it shares with the earlier St. Paul's Cathedral, M'dina. St. John's could be described as the Knights' own church, built by them between 1573 and 1577, and dedicated to St. John the Baptist. It remained the Conventual Church of the Order until 1798 and was granted Co-Cathedral status in 1816.

On approaching the building, the exterior strikes the visitor as singularly unremarkable, but what a different impression once inside! Originally just as plain, the interior was redesigned in Baroque style by the 17th century Italian artist, Mattia Preti, whose oil paintings depicting episodes from the life of John the Baptist adorn the splendid vaulted ceiling. The floor, too, is no less magnificent, paved with richly coloured marble tombstones of the Knights, each one decorated in mosaic with a Knight's particular coat of arms. Side chapels dedicated to various saints commemorate the different langues of the Order. Everything leads the eye to the dominant, raised high altar, made of marble, lapis lazuli and other semi-precious stones. It is, indeed, a masterpiece of a building.

If there is time, visit the oratory and museum. On display in the oratory is the now splendidly restored painting, *The Beheading of St. John the Baptist*, by Caravaggio (1573-1610), probably the finest painting to be seen in Malta. The museum itself contains an impressive collection of Flemish tapestries, as well as vestments, illuminated choir scores and remnants of the church silverware not stolen by Napoleon in 1798.

Moving on from churches but staying with the Knights, a visit to the Grand Master's Palace ought to be on the itinerary of every visitor. Though once the residence of the Grand Masters, most of it now houses the Maltese Parliament, but with part of it open to the public. Among the various exhibits the most notable are the strikingly beautiful 18th century Gobelin tapestries in the Small Council Chamber upstairs; further along from here, the Hall of St. Michael and St. George, with its frieze depicting the Great Siege; and the displays of armour lining both the upstairs corridors and also downstairs, taking pride of place in the Armoury itself (with one suit of armour worn by Grand Master Wignacourt weighing an incredible 50kg), along with an impressive collection of weapons from the 16th-18th centuries.

A spectacular view of the Three Cities where the Knights originally made their base can be seen from the Upper Barraka Gardens. To the far left is the entrance to the Grand Harbour, and across the harbour itself and immediately ahead are the two peninsulas around which the Three Cities were established, with Vittoriosa and Fort St. Angelo being very much the prominent features. Named Vittoriosa instead of Birgu to celebrate victory over the Turks, there is much here relating to the history of the Knights and a visit is recommended, but if there is time to visit only one of the cities, then without doubt this is the one to choose.

The Church of St. Lawrence stands proud along the waterfront. Dating back originally to the 11th century, it was in due course to become the Conventual Church of the Knights before they transferred to Valletta. Much restored by them, its current interior appearance in the Baroque style again owes much to the work of Lorenzo Gafà in the latter part of the 17th century. Though not always open, the

Grand harbour

adjacent chapel of St. Joseph contains a hat and sword of Jean de la Valette himself.

While in Vittoriosa make a point of visiting the Maritime Museum which contains many martitime mementoes from Roman to British times, including models of the Knights' ships as well as the modern Maltese fishing vessel, the *luzzu*. Nor should the Inquisitor's Palace be missed. Whilst maybe not as rigorous as the dreaded Spanish Inquisition, nevertheless the aim was to guard against heresy and keep the Knights on their moral toes! Here people of both sexes were imprisoned, tortured and executed. Restored since the Second World War when it was severely damaged by German bombing, dungeons, cells and courtrooms are open to view, and some of the rooms in the Palace are lavish indeed.

But Vittoriosa should not be left without a closer inspection of its most prominent landmark, Fort St. Angelo. It is possible that a temple was built on this spot in Phoenician times, followed by Greek and Roman ones, with the site eventually being developed as a fortress, particularly by the Knights when, during the Grand Siege, St. Angelo became their command post, just as it was also to become Royal Navy headquarters in 1912, as well as surviving the German bombing in 1942. A walk along the wharf towards the end of the promontory demomstrates the formidable scale of this imposing fortress standing guard over the Grand Harbour.

No visitor to Valletta should miss the opportunity of a cruise around the harbour, most of which begin from **Sliema**, a popular and fashionable resort, which at night-time provides wonderful views across Sliema Creek to the floodlit bastions of Valletta. Passing between Forts St. Elmo and Ricasoli, the cruise enters the harbour and the imagination is fired by the stirring events of the past, especially when it was the base of the Mediterranean fleet in World War II and destination for the Malta convoys battling their way through to maintain the survival of Malta and so pave the way for an allied victory.

Southern Malta

The visitor to Malta would be unwise to neglect the southern part of the island for here, among other places to be visited, are some of Malta's many remarkable prehistoric sites. Indeed, Malta's prehistory dates back to between 5000 and 4000 BC when immigrants whose way of life was predominantly agricultural came from Sicily. It is these people who are believed to be the first inhabitants of the island.

The cave at Ghar Dalam (the 'Cave of Darkness'), for example, dates back to these earliest times, about 4000 BC and along with its museum provides a glimpse into the island's prehistory. It seems likely that at one time a land bridge existed between North Africa, Malta and Sicily, becoming the means by which various animals found their way across, particularly dwarf elephants, bears and hippopotami, the remains of which, along with those of humans, were found in the cave. Many of these animal remains can be seen in the adjacent museum.

Not far away is the temple complex of Hagar Qim ('Standing Stones'). Somewhat younger than the Ghar Dalam site, Hagar Qim (about 3600 BC) is a marvel of prehistoric engineering. Built of soft limestone, the huge standing stones could more easily be decorated, but as a consequence have weathered badly. This impressive site, with its intricate design, prehistoric art and overall structure, bears testimony to a highly sophisticated society which originally planned and built it. If there is time, a short walk takes you to the Mnajdra Temples, set on a plateau overlooking the sea. Dating back to the same period as Hagar Qim, both these temple sites pre-date the Pyramids in Egypt by about 1000 years and appear to represent a community whose religion was based on fertility worship.

Both here and at **Tarxien** (just south from Valletta) will be found representations of the 'fat' goddess of fertility, sometimes unkindly called the Venus of Malta. The Tarxien temples are younger than the previously mentioned ones (about 3000-2400 BC) and depict the peak of pre-historic temple building, demonstrated by the precise cut of the stone slabs as well as some of the finest examples of pre-historic art. It is worth noting that the altars, statues and friezes are all copies and that the originals are displayed in the National Museum of Archaeology in Valletta, which repays a visit to view these and other artefacts of Maltese history.

The nearby Hypogeum was a vast underground burial place built on three levels and dating back to around 3000 BC. Such is its importance that it has been declared a world heritage site. Discovered accidentally by workmen in 1902, eventual excavations unearthed the remains of approximately 7000 people, along with pottery and jewellery. There is also an oracle chamber which suggests that rituals as well as burials took place. Due to damage caused by the breathing of visitors, numbers currently allowed in the site are strictly controlled, about 300 daily. A visit early in the day is therefore recommended. None the less, as with Tarxien, some of the finds here are on display in the Archaeological Museum in Valletta - a further reason for a visit!

Whilst in the southern part of the island, do take in two other places. One is the Blue Grotto where, particularly in the morning light, those who take the boat trip into the caves will be rewarded not only by the beautiful blue of the Mediterranean, but the varying hues of colour reflected back from the water into the caves themselves. The other place is **Marsaxlokk**, Malta's largest fishing village where, in the harbour, the traditional Maltese fishing boats, the luzzu, bob up and down on the water. It makes an excellent lunch stop.

Before moving on to Gozo, two other visits are highly recommended. The one is to 'The Malta Experience' in Valletta early on in any tour to the island. An audio-visual presentation, it depicts the colourful and stirring events which over the centuries have shaped Malta's past and present, so providing invaluable background information. The other is to one of the local festas which are held from May through till early October. These are colourful celebrations in many of the towns and villages, centred on the local band clubs. The churches are festooned with lights, flowers adorn the interior and the particular saint is paraded through the streets. The occasion is like an on-going street party and firework displays are an integral part of the festivities.

Gozo

About one-third the size of Malta, from which it is separated by a 5-mile wide channel, Gozo has a distinctly different feel to it. Much less cosmopolitan than parts of Malta, it is very much a farming and fishing community. More sparsely populated than its sister island, Gozo therefore has a more spacious feel to it. Fewer people, fewer roads, fewer vehicles all contribute to an atmosphere of rural tranquillity, which the Gozitans are anxious to keep in spite of the number of visitors. A journey of about 20 minutes from Cirkewwa in the north of Malta to Mgarr harbour on Gozo provides a most enjoyable day's excursion. What you see during your time on the island will depend on the particular itinerary selected by your tour company, but the following paragraphs pinpoint some of the main highlights.

Ggantija Temples: Believed to be the oldest free-standing monuments in the world and dating back to the period 3500-3000 BC, these temples are, therefore, of the utmost importance historically. As with the prehistoric temples on Malta, particularly those at Tarxien, the temples at Ggantija seem to have been places for the worship of a fertility goddess. Originally roofed-in, these two temples were constructed of limestone quarried from the hill opposite. The sheer effort involved in transferring the huge blocks of stone from the quarry to the temple site says much for their builders' engineering skills as well as their faith. As you wander around these temples you cannot help marvelling at the achievements of our prehistoric ancestors.

Ta' Pinu: This is a shrine of much pilgrimage, both now as well as in the past, a church within a church. The present building is in Romanesque style and dates from the 20th century and yet incorporates an original 16th century chapel named after a wealthy and devout local man whose nickname was Pinu. Three centuries later, in 1883, a peasant woman walking past the church is said to have heard a voice commanding her to go inside and say three Hail Marys. From then on it acquired a reputation for miracles and so became a centre of pilgrimage where people prayed for miracles, and in 1920 building began on the present vast, cathedral-like church.

Victoria (Rabat): Whatever else you see or don't see on a day excursion to Gozo, Victoria, the Capital, is a certainty. You may still hear it called by its Arab name, Rabat (meaning 'the city'). The main focal point of attraction for the visitor is the Citadel which, rather like M'dina's cathedral, dominates the landscape around. So, too, just as from M'dina's ramparts there are magnificent views across Malta, from here also is a splendid vista over Gozo. The area of the Citadel is covered with narrow streets containing various places of interest like the Armoury and the Folklore Museum. But by far the main point of interest is the 17th century Cathedral of the Assumption, designed by the Maltese architect of M'dina cathedral, Lorenzo Gafà. Though Baroque in style, this does not give the impression of being over-ostentatious as do some others. As well as the colourful floor decorated with the tombstones of bishops and priests, be sure to notice a remarkable trick of the eye. Though a dome was originally intended it was never finally completed. To remedy this defect a Sicilian painter named Antonio Manuele was commisioned in 1739 to paint an area of the flat ceiling to give the effect of its being a dome. Stand beneath it and look upwards and it has all the appearance of being a dome, so cleverly did the artist design it. There is also a Cathedral Museum, with a collection of vestments, silverware and paintings.

In addition to these main sites there are a number of very pleasant ports of call, such as the fishing village of **Malsaforn** and the delightful bay of **Xlendi**, both making excellent lunch venues. Other possible stops are Calypso's Cave, where Ulysses is said to have had a dalliance with the nymph, Calypso, and the Azure Window and the Fungus Rock, the Window being a natural tunnel-like rock formation linking the open sea with a deep blue-coloured lagoon. The Rock is so called because the Knights valued a fungus growing on it with which they treated intestinal disorders! The above description of Gozo has assumed a day excursion from Malta, which is what the

The Grand Master's Barge

vast majority of visitors do. It is possible, however, to combine a stay on Malta with a few nights on Gozo.

And finally ......

'*The Kappillan of Malta*', by Nicholas Monsarrat. Though these days it can be bought only in Malta, either at the airport or in the shops in Valletta and Sliema, it is well worth obtaining. Set against the background of the Second World War it is the story of a priest who, during the crucial period 1940-1942, holds his people together in the underground catacombs of Malta. Although a work of fiction, the story is interspersed with reflections on some of the great events of Maltese history, such as the arrival of St. Paul, and the Great Siege of 1565. A moving testimony to the island's suffering and courage, it provides a fascinating glimpse into the Malta of World War II.

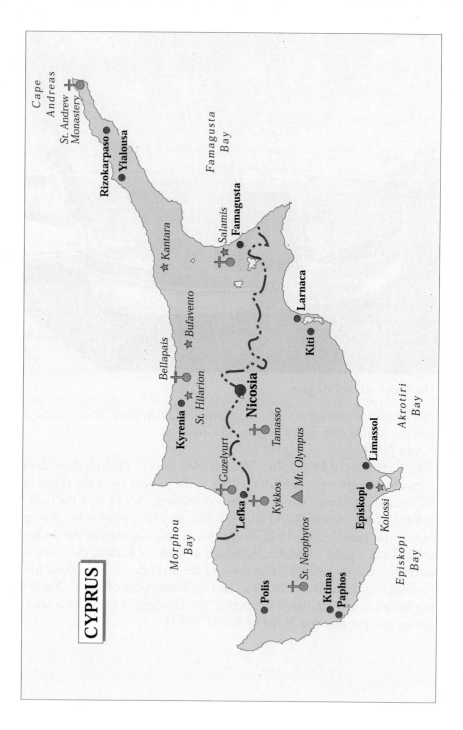

St Paul in Cyprus

The strategic position of Cyprus, just 40 miles south of Turkey and 60 miles west of the Syrian coastline, has always ensured its importance in world history. There are signs of settlements from the Stone Age, some going back as far as 7000 BC, and it is no surprise that the Island plays a significant part in the development of Christianity.

St Paul arrived, together with Barnabas and John Mark, (he of St Mark's Gospel) in AD 45, having set out from Antioch and arriving in Salamis, where Barnabas had been born. They travelled on to Paphos, where Paul converted the Roman pro-consul, and before leaving to sail to Attalia in Turkey they had established a thriving Church. Cyprus was also a natural stopping place for the early pilgrims to the Holy Land including the first of them all, St Helena, mother of Constantine, who had by then become the first of the Christian Emperors of Rome. She was there about AD 327 and famously rid the peninsular of Akrotiri of a plague of snakes by letting loose a thousand cats.

It was also a staging post for the Crusaders on their way to their major port of Acre, on the Mediterranean coast of what is now Israel. Richard the First (the Lionheart) of England came ashore from being shipwrecked in battle, to conquer the island and marry Berengaria, who thus became Queen of England. That was in 1191, and he in turn ceded it to the Knights Templar, one of whom, Guy de Lusignan, a deposed King of Jerusalem, was to have a more lasting effect on the development of the island. When the Crusaders lost their last remaining stronghold in the Holy Land, the port of Acre, in 1291, they retreated to Cyprus, reduced the natives to serfdom and built the great castles of St Hilarion, Buffavento and Kantara on the mountaintops of the Kyrenia Range. They administered the island from the great castle at Kolossi, near Limassol.

This range of mountains is one of the three main physical features, as it runs almost the length of the Island in what is now North Cyprus. The Troodos Mountains to the south, dominated by Mt Olympus (6400ft) cover nearly half the total area of the Island, and in between is the fertile plain of Mesaoria, from which comes most of the citrus fruit which (after tourism) is one of the great mainstays of the economy.

The early Christian settlers, many of them refugees from the conquering Arabs in the Holy Land, were responsible for the building of hundreds of churches and monasteries, many of them beautifully adorned with mosaics and frescoes which are still a joy to see.

Cyprus bears all the marks of so many invasions, battles, and civilisations. Phoenicians, Assyrians, Greeks, Egyptians, Persians and Romans have all left their stamp, and have provided the visitor with a wealth of history, architecture and art at which to marvel. Turkish Islamic rule over 300 years led up to British rule from 1878 until independence was granted in 1960. There came further disruption with the fight over Enosis, union with Greece, which led to the invasion by Turkey in 1974, the occupation of almost 40% of the island and the creation of the Turkish Republic of North Cyprus, of which more in the next section.

The lion of St. Mark guards the citadel of Famagusta

South Cyprus

Paphos

Possibly the most attractive of the resorts, built around a picturesque harbour, where pelicans wander among the café tables. Paphos is also important to the historian and the Christian visitor, for it was here that Paul and Barnabas had their significant clash with authority in the shape of the Roman pro-consul, Sergius Paulus, who was under the influence of a Jewish sorcerer called Elymas (or Bar-Jesus). The story is told in Acts 13 of how Elymas tried to turn the consul away from the new Christian faith, but was blinded by Paul, and the consul was converted. This was a significant step in the penetration of Christianity into the Roman Empire and also led to the dominance of the new faith in Cyprus itself, which by the 4th century had a great preponderance of places of worship.

In Paphos you will be shown the "St Paul Pillar" which is, according to legend (but not the Biblical story), where Paul was tied and given 39 lashes. It was the centre of Roman authority, having been largely re-built after an earthquake of 15BC The Romans stayed until more earthquakes in the 4th century marked the decline of their power. In the meantime, however, they had built a large number of palatial villas with some wonderful mosaics, many of which can still be seen. Four of these villas in particular, those of Dionysos, Theseus, Aeon and Orpheus, are in a compact area quite near the harbour and should not be missed. Also in the same area are other remains from the Roman era including the Odeon, a restored theatre from the 2nd century, the Asklepeion, parts of the Agora, and the Acropolis, now topped by a lighthouse.

All of this is within the area bounded by the old City Walls, which are partly excavated, and which contained the area known as Nea (or new) Paphos, running down to the port area. On the other side of the main Avenue Apostolos Pavlou, which leads down to the harbour, are the sites of interest to the Christian visitor, in particular St Paul's Pillar, and the adjoining Church of the Blessed Virgin Mary (Ayia Kyriaki Chrysopolitissa), a 16th century building on the site of a

The church of St Paraskevi at Yeroskipos

much earlier church, the foundations of which can be seen. This was a very large building and there are some mosaics which date from the 4th century and some signs of a later, Gothic church. The present church is shared by English Anglican and Catholic congregations, who hold regular services at the invitation of the local Orthodox priest.

There are two castles in Paphos which should be seen. The Byzantine Castle, which is passed en route to the Roman Villas, is partly excavated and restored and dates from the 7th century AD. It once had 40 columns but was almost destroyed by the earthquake of 1222. Before that it had been surrendered to Richard the Lionheart in 1191. It is an open site but is not well maintained and care is needed when visiting it. The other Castle, or medieval fort, dominates the harbour and owes its present form to the Turks, who built it in 1592. Climbing to the top provides a splendid view, but there is little inside of interest today.

The main part of Paphos town is also known as Ktima, and lies uphill about a mile from the harbour. It has all the modern commercial facilities and also houses the major Museums. The Paphos

The monastery of St Neophytos

District Museum is worth keeping an eye on as it has a continually growing collection of archaeological finds, as digs continue in the area. The Eliiades Collection is a private collection lovingly put together in an old private house, and includes some fossils which go back millions of years. You may need an appointment to visit.

Between the old and new towns, a signed turning off leads to the Tombs of the Kings, an impressive group of burial chambers, some colonnaded, which date from the 3rd-2nd centuries BC. Although there were no Kings of Cyprus at the time they were used, they must have been the final resting place of some very important people. Later they were also used as Christian burial grounds and as refuges.

Places near Paphos

On the coast road towards Limassol, the little village of **Yeroskipos**, two miles east, is worth a stop, if only to purchase or sample the Turkish delight for which it is famous (though they don't call it Turkish any more) . But it also has a small Byzantine church, that of

Ayia Paraskevi, which is probably one of the most interesting and attractive on the island. It dates from the 11th century, has five domes, and some marvellous frescoes and icons. The frecoes depict various Biblical scenes and mainly date from the 15th century. There is a delightful little Folk Museum nearby.

Along this road you can hardly fail to notice that the legend of **Aphrodite** is one upon which Cyprus depends for much of its folklore. Certainly all Cypriots will tell you that their island is the true home of the goddess of love and beauty, from whom springs the very essence of the land. You will come first to the Temple of Aphrodite at Paleapaphos, (now Kouklia) which was a very large place of worship, but a great deal has yet to be excavated. The site goes back to the 12th century BC. The temple was one of the most important places of pilgrimage in the ancient world, and was at one time a City Kingdom of itself. There is evidence of two Sanctuaries and some fragments of a mosaic floor. Further along the road, at Petra Tou Romiou, is the site known as Aphrodite's Birthplace, some rock formations on the beach where the goddess is said to have emerged from the waves. It is a very lovely situation, but even lovelier is the site of the Baths of Aphrodite, near Polis on the northern coast on the Akamas Peninsular. It will be about an hour's drive north from Paphos on a road which nearer the spot is not a good one, but well worth the effort. There are springs and pools set in woodland above the sea, shaded by a fig tree - the whole site is one of the most scenic in all of Cyprus and its romantic associations can only enhance the views. You can follow a walking trail for some 5 miles with stunning views of the coast, to the legendary Fontana Amorosa.

Another worth while trip from Paphos is to the Monastery of Ayios Neophytos, 6 miles away, and set on the mountain side where the saint, upon arriving in 1159, dug caves in the rock to lead the life of a hermit. He was a preacher and writer, and some of his manuscripts survive in the monastery. You can visit the Enclistra, or Hermitage, which contains the tomb of the saint and is covered with magnificent frescoes, some depicting the saint himself, with the archangels Michael and Gabriel.

The Troodos Mountains and Monasteries

It is well worth hiring a car for a day to take a ride into the mountains both for the scenery, which is often stunning, but also to see some

Frescoes cover the ceiling and Walls of the hermi's cave at St Neophytos Monastery

of the finest icons and frescoes of Cyprus in the nine Byzantine churches which were designated by UNESCO as among the finest World Heritage sites. The mountain range covers nearly half of the total area of Cyprus and is one of the two major geographical features of the island (the other is the Kyrenia range in northern Cyprus). It reaches its pinnacle in Mt Olympus at 6400ft. There can be winter skiing on the slopes and warm sunshine on the coast below, all on the same day at certain times of the year. But let us return to the heritage sites, most of which are grouped around the main resort, Pano Platres, which is at 3700ft and under an hour's drive from the coast. About 5 miles away is the Troodhitissa Monastery, hidden in deep forests, and built in 1250 by two hermit monks after they saw a vision of the Virgin Mary and preserved an icon of the Virgin through several fires and other tribulations. The present building dates from the 19th century. There is an annual festival on 15-16th August to celebrate the salvation of the icon. Kykko Monastery, the largest of the group, is reached by a tortuous road deep into the mountains, and again owes its origin to a hermit monk in AD 1100 who was presented with an icon of the Virgin Mary said to have been painted by St Luke. The icon miraculously survived several fires and is now covered in silver. It is said to have magical rain-bringing powers and so is much venerated by the local farmers. Quite near here is the tomb of Archbishop Makarios, set among pine trees overlooking a grand panorama.

To visit all of the churches on the UNESCO list would takve several days; additionally, for many of them it is necessary to first find the keyholder to let you in. However, the most famous, and probably the finest, is that of St Nicholas of the Roof (Agios Nicholaos tis Stegis) near the resort of Kakopetria. Its roof is of reddish brown wood shingles. It occupies a lovely garden setting and the interior boasts some exceptionally fine frescoes, of varying date from the 11th to the 17th centuries The style of painting appears less rigid than most of this kind and are the more attractive for it.

Limassol and area

Limassol is a major resort with numerous hotels and a very long sea front - at least 5 miles of it. For all that, it is not so attractive as Paphos, and one has the feeling that the authorities could have done a great deal more to enhance the seafront with gardens and other facilities. It is the largest port - you can take short cruises to Israel or Egypt from here - and the second biggest city (after Nicosia). More noted for its night life, wineries and fine beaches (not to mention a zoo), than for its history, Limassol does none the less have a good deal to offer the serious sightseer. At Amathus, on the edge of the town, was an ancient settlement, now but a collection of old stones, where Berengaria, fiancee of Richard the Lionheart, was shipwrecked and blown ashore. The local ruler was less than welcoming, so Richard had to take to arms to rescue his beloved, whom he then married in the local castle, on the 12th May 1191. Whilst he was about it, he captured the rest of the island too, but later sold it to the Knights Templar, who in turn passed it to the Lusignans. The Knights of St John made it their headquarters and it became a thriving city.

The present Castle dates from 1571 when it was rebuilt by the Turks, and it served as HQ for the British Army in World War II. Nowadays it is virtually empty but you can see the Great Hall and some cells from the time it was used as a prison. There is a very good view of the harbour from the roof. The Medieval Museum is a small but interesting collection within the castle, and there is also the Limassol District Museum behind the main Public Gardens, which has a good collection of archaeological finds through pottery to jewellery.

Places to visist near Limassol

A large part of the **Akrotiri Peninsular,** which almost adjoins Limassol, is British Sovereign Territory, being part of the military base ceded to Britain as part of the Independence arrangements for Cyprus made in 1960. Much of it is thus out of bounds, but the Ladies Mile beach is excellent and almost deserted, and the salt lake is a magnet for bird watchers and is populated by migrating flamingoes during the winter months. The Church of Ayios Nikolaos of the Cats is a small monastic establishment which was founded in AD325 after a visit from St Helena. The story is that the whole area was over-run by poisonous snakes, and Helena brought a large number of cats, which rapidly cleared the menace.

Back on the coast road towards Paphos is the imposing Kolossi Castle, the most important medieval castle in Cyprus. Isaac Comnenos, the local commander who was defeated by Richard the Lionheart, held court here and it then passed to the order of St John, whose authority operated through a feudal system of Commanderies, each covering a number of villages. Their huge estates included sugar cane production and vineyards, from which came the famous sweet red wine, Commandaria, which remains a favourite today. The Lusignan Coat of Arms is to be seen on the eastern side of the castle with four shields depicting the Kingdoms of Jerusalem, Cyprus and Armenia, plus the fleur de lys emblem of the Grand Commander, Luis de Magnac who oversaw the construction. The present edifice is just the keep from the 15th century, and it is entered by a stone bridge across the moat. The interior is rather stark, but the scale of the rooms is vast. Further along the coast, at Episkopi, the next stop is at Kourion, a major attraction for all tourists. It is a vast site, and what you can see today is mostly of Roman origin, though its beginnings as a settlement were as far back as the 12th century BC. There are three main areas, the ancient city, the stadium and the Temple of Apollo. There is a Christian basilica, dating from the 5th century, and a most impressive theatre, overlooking the sea, which was only discovered and excavated in 1935. It now seats 3500 people for performances and concerts in a truly awe-inspiring setting. There is a great deal to see here, including a roman villa, baths, many mosaics, and the stadium, which has been partly re-built. The Temple, also partly re-constructed, has a grand flight of steps and a colonnaded portico, but like much of this site it was badly ravaged by earthquakes in the 4th century. When excavations began in earnest in 1876, they were financed by an American consul-general, and vast treasures of gold and silver jewellery were found, and immediately sent to the Metropolitan Museum in New York.

Places to see in and around Nicosia

The divided capital of Cyprus does not have a great deal to attract the tourist but it has a pleasant old town, known as Laiki Yitonia, which has been well restored with many arts and craft shops, cafes and galleries. It has both an Orthodox Cathedral (17th century) and an Anglican one, a Byzantine Museum and a Folk Art Museum, with a pricelsss collection of icons in the former, and some excellent pottery, lace and embroidery in the latter.

Some other places to see

Larnanca: The third largest city and a major resort, Larnaca also has the main airport of Cyprus. The two main reasons for visiting it are the Church of St Lazarus and the Pierides Museum. The Church is dedicated to the patron Saint of Larnaca, as he supposedly sailed into the port following his resurrection by Jesus at Bethany. He became a Bishop, died and was buried here, his tomb being discovered in AD 890. The first church was built over the tomb in the 9th century but has been rebuilt several times. The present one is a curious mixture of Romanesque, Gothic and Byzantine styles, with a 19th century Bell Tower. There are some remarkable icons, naturally depicting the Raising of Lazarus. The Pierides Museum started as a private collection in a private home, and contains a huge collection of archaeological treasures from Neolithic times, including statuettes, pottery and Roman glass. It is one of the best museums in Cyprus.

Lefkara: A pretty village in the hills between Limassol and Larnaca. At around 2500ft it also supplies wonderful views, but its main claim to fame is for the making of lace. The village houses are more reminiscent of Spain with their balconies, as are the narrow streets and courtyards. A most photogenic place. Leonardo da Vinci, on a visit to Cyprus

in 1481 is said to have bought lace here for the altar in Milan Cathedral.
Kiti: Some 7 miles south of Larnaca, beyond the airport, Kiti is a small
village known mainly for its Church, Panayia Angeloktisti (Church of
the Virgin Mary, Built by the Angels) parts of which date back to the
5th century. Though it has been re-built several times, it is one of the
oldest on the island, and its major treasure is a 6th century mosaic
depicting the Virgin Mary holding the baby Jesus, with the Archangels
Michael and Gabriel in attendance. The quality of this work still shows
and it is claimed as one of the finest mosaics in the world.

Monastery of Ayios Herakleidos: South of Nicosia, in a garden setting near Tamassos (where there are some Royal Tombs), this church
is dedicated to Herakleidos, who was chosen by Paul and Barnabas as
their guide and companion. They appointed him Bishop, but after
their departure from Cyprus, he was killed by pagans and buried here.
His tomb is in the crypt and his skull is kept in a gold casket. The
church was restored in the 18th century and is also a nunnery where
the incumbents produce rose jams and marzipan.

CROSSING THE LINE

Crossing from the Greek part to the Turkish (North Cyprus) part of the Island is
currently possible only at one point in Nicosia, near the former Ledra Palace
Hotel. Neither side makes it easy, and you can cross only for a day, and must
return by 5pm. There is no provision for groups to cross, but there are tour com-
panies on the Turkish side that will arrange coaches and guides for tours in the
north. Passports are necessary but not visas. At the time of writing there are
"Proximity Talks" in progress between the two sides which may result in some
easing of restrictions enabling tourists to transit from one side to the other
more easily. Crossing from North to South is not at present possible.

North Cyprus

The events leading up to the division of Cyprus in 1974 would takean-other book of this length to describe.

Suffice it to say that Turkish forces occupied some 37% of the land area of the island and set up the Turkish Republic of North Cyprus, which is autonomous from mainland Turkey, though heavily subsidised by it. The country is recognised as such only by Turkey, and a number of international sanctions remain in force at the time of writing, affecting visitors mainly in difficulties of access. There are no direct flights, all have to come via Turkey, usually stopping at Istanbul or Izmir before travelling on to the North Cyprus airport at Ercan. There are ferry services from the mainland, from Mersin to Famagusta and from Tasucu to Kyrenia, but not daily, and schedules vary with the seasons.

North Cyprus has some 200,000 inhabitants, mainly concentrated in the three main towns of Nicosia (which is divided between north and south and is known locally as Lefkosa) , Famagusta (Gazimagusa in Turkish), and Kyrenia (Girne). It also has the bulk of the Mesaoria Plain, a large area of flat land largely uncultivated, and the Kyrenia Mountain range, the feature of which is the "Five Fingered Mountain" (Pentadaktylos) which rises to some 2400ft and has an eye-catching silhouette. The other feature is the long finger of the Karpasia Peninsular which stretches north-eastwards to the sea by the Monastery of Apostolos Andreas, for it is said that St Andrew, on his way to Palestine, struck a rock from which gushed a spring, the water of which had healing powers.

For the Christian visitor, the major points of interest are the remains at Salamis, and the nearby Monastery of St Barnabas, the lovely Abbey at Bellapais, the Crusader Castles, and some monasteries and churches which remain. We shall visit each of these in turn, but perhaps we should start by advising all those intending a visit to first read the book "Bitter Lemons" by Lawrence Durrell (published in 1957) which tells of his efforts to set up home in the village of Bellapais, among both Greek and Turkish people, who managed to live together in reasonable harmony for generations until the radicals on both sides forced the great divide. There are occasional attempts to bring the two sides

ABOVE: *Salamis*
BELOW: *The Abbey of Bellapais*

93

together, but the problems seem to be as intractable as those between Arab and Jew, and so we have yet another north/south split which we have to live with in sorrow.

The essential sightseeing in North Cyprus would take up no more than two days, but a longer stay can be very pleasant as the beaches here are excellent and there is plenty of character about the main towns and resorts, which would repay a week's holidaymaking. Taxis and car hire are cheap, as is eating out in the vast selection of restaurants, and hotel quality is good. The currency here is Turkish lire and the languages used are Turkish and English.

Places to visit

The major place of interest to those interested in history, and especially in tracing the early Church, is **Salamis**. The site is a few miles from Famagusta and covers a large area, about 1 square mile. It was a Greco-Roman city, with some 100,000 inhabitants at its height, and most important of the city-kingdoms of Cyprus in the pre-Christian era. But its history goes back at least to the 11th century BC when it was populated by Achaean and Anatolian settlers. In Roman times it was known as Constantia, after being re-built by Constantine following an earthquake, and most of what remains today is of Roman construction. When Paul and Barnabas were here it is reasonable to assume that they preached in the colonnaded Forum, and though much of the site has still to be excavated it is possible to visualise the streets, markets, and baths of the Roman city. The most impressive remains are of the Gymnasium, Palaestra, and the Theatre, which has been partly reconstructed to house concerts and other events. There are marble columns and Roman statues (mostly headless), which make this a very impressive site and one of the highlights of a visit to Northern Cyprus.

We know that Paul and Barnabas moved on from Salamis to Paphos, and sailed from there to Perga, but we also know that Barnabas returned to Salamis at a later time, for he was martyred and buried under a carob tree at a site about a mile away. With him was buried a copy of Matthew's Gospel which he had always carried with him, and when his tomb was discovered and re-opened at the order of Bishop Anticituis some 432 years later, it was found that the Gospel was intact. The tomb is now in a small chapel in an olive grove some 200 meters from the Monastery of St Barnabas, which is a more modern institution (from 1756), and which contains a fresco of the Barnabas story and a collection of icons. There is also here a small Archaeological Museum, with a good collection of pottery and other items from the early bronze age up to 1200 BC. In the same area, for this was clearly a burial ground of the time, are the Royal Tombs. Around 20 burial chambers can be seen, though up to 50 have been excavated and it is estimated that there are nearly 1000 altogether. They date from the Mycean era and a point of interest is that a number of apparent noblemen were buried with their horses, including harness, and chariots. One of the tombs (No.50) is that of St. Catherine, a daughter of another Constantine, one of the Kings of Salamis, which is built like a church. She lived, was imprisoned for her faith, and died there in the 3rd century.

Famagusta: A fortified town with immense walls and bastions, built by the Lusignans and strenghtened by the Venetians. It became one of the major centres of Christianity after refugees arrived from the Holy Land from 1291 following the defeat of the Crusaders. They built no less than 365 churches, and substantial remnants of quite a number of them remain today. The major one is the Cathedral of St Nicholas, which is now better known, and used, as the Lala Mustafa Pasha Mosque. It was built in true Gothic style in the 4th century and the Lusignan Kings of Cyprus came here to be crowned also as Kings of Jerusalem. The Gothic front is surmounted by a minaret. The former Venetian Palace, opposite the cathedral, is now in part a car park, one of the signs of a rather sad decline in the fortunes of Famagusta, which seems not to have recovered from the departure of the large Greek Cypriot population in 1974. A substantial section of the town is now a part of the no-man's-land between the two communities. Most of the remaining churches have been fenced off and are not accessible, though traces of some fine Gothic stonework can be seen on many of them. Parts of the old fortifications are now being put to good use as museums or arts centres, but the one of greatest interest is the Citadel, also known as Othello's Tower, which has a splendid 14th century Gothic Hall. Over the gateway is the Winged Lion of St Mark, the symbol Famagusta has taken to itself. It is generally thought that Shakespeare took the story of his Moorish King from the life of one Christoforo Moro, a Governor of Cyprus in the 16th century.

Kyrenia or Girne: The other main resort, on the northern coast, and

The harbour at Kyrenia

probably the best centre for a stay. It is set around a most attractive harbour, which is dominated by the castle, a massive bastion, rebuilt by the Lusignans and again further strengthened by the Venetians. The locals boast that in all its history their castle has never been taken by assault. The castle contains a Byzantine chapel, and museum dedicated to the Kyrenia Ship, the remains of a 4th century BC Greek vessel salvaged off the coast, one of the oldest vessels ever discovered and salvaged in this way.

Of the Crusader Castles, the most accessible is St. Hilarion, which overlooks Kyrenia. Like the others, it was built in the 10th century over the grave of the Saint who had lived a hermit's life on the mountain until his death in the 8th century AD. It became a stronghold and an essential part of the Crusader defence of the island. They could send signals to each of these mountain top castles and from them survey virtually a whole swathe of the island. St. Hilarion is built on three levels and it needs quite a lot of climbing to see it all, but the views to the coast are stunning. Buffavento, to the east of Kyrenia is the highest, set at 3100ft, and was used mainly as a prison, but was largely destroyed by the Venetians in the 15th century. The third castle, Kantara, stands at just over 2000ft and is some 40 miles to the east of Kyrenia.

Bellapais: Its Abbey will be a highlight of any visit, especially for those who have read and delighted in Laurence Durrell's "Bitter Lemons". The Tree of Idleness, which now stands within the garden of a restaurant of the same name, cannot be the same one he described, but the atmosphere is there, even to the sense of indolence in the afternoon sun. The Abbey sits on its cliff top, some 700 ft above the sea and with a stunning view from its terrace. It dates from the 13th century when it was founded by the Augustinian order, and is built in Gothic style, with cloisters and a great vaulted refectory with a lovely rose window. The church itself has a number of very old icons and the whole setting responds to the name of Abbaye de la Paix, Abbey of Peace. It might just be a symbol for the bringing back together of the two communities that once lived here, and on the whole of Cyprus, in peace with each other.

Other places to visit in North Cyprus

Nicosia (Lefkosa in Turkish): The Turkish Quarter of the capital does not have a great deal of interest, though the Venetian walls with their bastions and gateways are a feature. The major interest for us lies in the former St. Sophia Cathedral, which is now the Selimiye Mosque. It dates from 1298-1312 and the grandeur of the Gothic interior, with its columns, is still redolent of the Christian cathedrals of this time. It has some grave stones from the Christian era. It became a mosque in 1576, and the Gothic west front is surmounted by two minarets. Next door is another former church, that of St. George, which has become a bazaar, and at the rear is the former Archbishop's House which is being used as a Lapidiary Museum, with fine examples of stone work. Yet another old church in the same area is that of St Nicholas of the English which has a finely worked Gothic Arch.

The Monastery of St Andrew (Apostollos Andreas): At the very end of the Karpas Peninsular (the "pan-handle" of Cyprus), and is a two hour drive from Limassol, through some attractive countryside. On arrival, the site and the building are something of a disappointment, but an old lady will open the Church which has some very ancient icons. The story is that St Andrew, the Patron Saint of travellers, was sailing back to Palestine when his ship was wrecked in the narrow channel here, partly because its captain had lost the sight of one eye. Andrew came ashore, thrust his stave into the rock, and out poured a stream of water, which proved to have healing powers, for the captain recovered his sight.

But if you are interested to follow the stories of the saints, you may like to go to the other end of the Island. Near Lefke are the ruins of Soli, which was a great Roman city of the 6th century BC. An amphitheatre and a Christian basilica are among the sites excavated. But also in that area, in the town of Guzelyurt, is the Monastery of St. Mamas. He was a stubborn man who refused to pay his taxes, and the Governor sent troops to bring him to Court in the capital. On the way they came across a lamb being set upon by a lion. Mamas sent the lion away, took the lamb in his arms, and carried it to the safety of the town. The Governor was so impressed, he forgave Mamas and released him from liability to pay taxes for the rest of his life. St Mamas thus became the Patron saint of tax dodgers !

Salamis

A view at the end of every street - Athens

Postscript

Jerusalem to Rome - Jew to Gentile

A book about "The Lands of St. Paul", though on one level tracing the geographical travels of a very remarkable man, must also seek to represent something of the driving imperative behind them. Though it is beyond the scope of this volume to deal in any detail with the ultimate destination, Rome, yet given the extent of St. Paul's ministry from Jerusalem to Rome, it is only fitting to conclude with some brief reference to his time in the capital of the Empire. After all, it was the Council of Jerusalem, described in Acts 15, which provided the impetus for the Apostle and his companions to take the Christian message beyond the boundaries of Judaism.

The great dilemma facing the early church in that council was not merely to do with practicalities about the admission of Gentiles into the church, but with the very principle itself - should Gentiles be allowed to enter? That was the crux of the debate. Now if by some stretch of the imagination we can contemplate a negative answer to that question, then it is just conceivable that Christianity might have become little more than a localised sect within Palestine. However, once it was acknowledged that Gentiles as well as Jews had received the gift of the Holy Spirit, then the way was open for Paul to lead the advance from Jerusalem and take the Christian Gospel across barriers of race, religion, language and culture, so that far from being a localised phenomenon, it was to become a world-wide, all-embracing dynamic movement. From Jerusalem to Rome, from Jew to Gentile, such was its breadth.

After sailing from Malta, Paul and his companions put ashore in Italy at Puteoli, now Pozzuoli, the port near Naples then serving Rome. On their way into the capital by the Via Appia, they were greeted and offered hospitality by local believers. Acts 26: 13-31 deals with Paul's time in the city.

During his two years here, though under some kind of liberal house arrest, Paul had enough freedom to continue his preaching and teaching among both the Jewish and Gentile communities. How or when he was put to death in the city we do not know. Whether it was the culmination of his previous trials or some new accusation against him, we can only surmise. Maybe the details do not matter.

What is of paramount importance is the symbolism of Rome as the centre of the Gentile world, to which Paul had given so much of his devotion and energy. By taking the Christian message from Jerusalem to Rome he became the catalyst by which the world vision of Pentecost in Acts 2 became a reality. So whether we follow his steps in Turkey, Greece, Malta or Cyprus, or even, if we are fortunate, at some stage to all four, we are not merely travellers but pilgrims who hopefully will be infected by something of his faith, vision and commitment.

JRG
DH

Index of Place Names

Notes